The

D1586332

111 Places
in Amsterdam
That You
Shouldn't Miss

111

emons:

© Emons Verlag GmbH
All rights reserved
© All photographs: Thomas Fuchs, except
chapter 1: 2theLoo; chapter 2: Robert Bot (Link2Party);
chapter 6: Cassander Eeftink Schattenkerk; chapter 9: Aviodrome;
chapter 12: Battello; chapter 14: Hans Mooren; chapter 39: Glowgolf;
chapter 60: Marriage for a Day; chapter 63: Hans van den Bogaard;
chapter 70: Annetje Praag – van Sigaar; chapter 81: Erik Smits;
chapter 88: Alltournative; chapter 96: Torpedo Theater; chapter 99: Foto De Boer;
chapter 104: Arjen Veldt; chapter 105: Ski-Inn
English translation: John Sykes
Design: Eva Kraskes, based on a design
by Lübbeke | Naumann | Thoben
Maps: altancicek.design, www.altancicek.de
Printing and binding: CPI – Clausen & Bosse, Leck
Printed in Germany 2017
ISBN 978-3-7408-0023-9

Did you enjoy it? Do you want more?
Join us in uncovering new places around the world on:
www.111places.com

Foreword

Amsterdam may not be among the biggest cities in the world, but its numbers are impressive nonetheless. The city is home to people of more than 180 nationalities, who, for the most part get along astonishingly well. Amsterdam is proud of its 165 canals; hence, the nickname "Venice of the North." The phrase was coined by some Italian guy in the 16th century, so we can assume it was meant as compliment. Water was and is important for the city, as you can tell by the fact that it hosts 1,281 bridges, nine ferries and 2,500 houseboats. Windmills, another thing closely associated with the Netherlands, are actually rather scarce (the city has only eight), but the number of bicycles meets expectation: 881,000. Statistically speaking, every citizen owns at least one.

When I wrote this book, I tried to recall when I first came to town a long time ago. What would have helped me to separate the wheat from the chaff as quickly as possible? What would have helped me get the whole picture? So I was looking for the unexpected aspects, but of course I could not omit the famous sites. For this book, I have tried to find place, stories, and facts that are not so well known.

And there is another thing: even though Amsterdammers like to travel far and wide (New York City was founded as Nieuw Amsterdam, after all), they are not always fond of typical tourists. But this book provides all the information you need to get along swimmingly with the locals.

You will find a selection of 111 places, covering the sites for which Amsterdam is famous (and sometimes infamous) and some hidden gems as well. If you feel encouraged to venture out and find the must-see spots on your own, please do. This book should provide more than enough places to start. Amsterdam is a city of individualists. So if you want to make the most of your trip, be as individualistic as you like. And first and foremost: have fun.

Thomas Fuchs

111 Places

1__2theloo
Relief for an incontinent continent

We will begin with a somewhat delicate matter. You can hardly overlook them in the city centre, and even if you do not notice them, the smell will attract your attention: small green urinals where men can relieve themselves. Which they do too seldom. Undisciplined urinating on the street is a major problem in Amsterdam. It is estimated that 35,000 litres per year trickle into the ground in an unapproved way. In view of such a great quantity, you could say that the city, built on wooden piles, is irrigated from above as well as from below. Whether this amount of urine is also a threat to the fabric of the city – well, that's for others to decide, but it is at the very least a public nuisance.

Despite a popular belief to the contrary, 'wildplassen' is not allowed in Amsterdam. According to the APV (Algemene Plaatselijke Verordening, General Local Regulations), paragraph 5.1, this is an offence, forbidden and subject to a fine. Now that's food for thought: in a city where almost everything is tolerated, some things are simply prohibited. But it is equally clear that the police would have too much to do if they had to chase after every offender whose bladder was bursting.

A different approach is taken by a company called 2theloo, which is making the matter of relieving yourself into something like an event. The facilities are clean, amusingly designed and conceived so that they can easily be installed in train stations, petrol stations and shopping centres.

Alongside this basic business, 2theloo also sells toiletry items in the cubicles. You can even get a cup of coffee in some of them. Their water closets now stand in more than 80 locations, not only in Holland but spread across the whole continent. The graphic design is adapted to the sites. The adornment in Amsterdam is – 'of course', it is tempting to say – Rembrandt's *Night Watch*.

Address Kalverstraat 126 (Flagship-Store), NL-1012 PK Amsterdam (Centrum) | Getting there Tram 4, 19, 16, 24 or 25 to Spui | Hours Mon–Fri 9am–6pm | Tip In front of the Grand Hotel at Oudezijds Voorburgwal 197 is a urinal designed by the Amsterdam School that is now a listed monument.

2__Air
Today's iT experts

Air is one of the trendiest clubs in the city. Its managers are proud of the varied programme and the interior fittings, which were specially commissioned from a fashionable Dutch designer.

The whole place has been divided into different sections and designed so that the atmosphere is always pleasant, regardless of whether 100 or 1,000 guests are present. Air also claims to have a heart for a wide range of people – something that cannot be taken for granted in the age of door bitches. But the most striking thing about Air is that – as far as Amsterdam's nightlife is concerned – it stands on a famous, even holy site.

The place where Air admits its guests today was once iT. In the nineties, back in the last century (the last millennium, even) this club was thought unique in the world. It was in the same league as Studio 54 in New York, or even higher, in a class of its own. Whereas Studio 54 boasted about its celebrity guests, at iT this went without saying, and beyond that, the star of the show here was the clientele.

An insider once described the crowd as 'homos, hoeren & shoarmaboeren' (for those who don't speak Dutch, let's translate that literally as 'homos, whores & shawarma-farmers'). In its glory days, rumours circulated about all kinds of excesses at the club, and its motto was that everyone should find their own kind of happiness. The atmosphere at iT was considered so free and easy that even heterosexuals could simply be themselves.

However, it lies in the nature of excesses that the ecstasy is followed by the hangover. The operators of the joint were proud to be one of the first in the city to have a dark room, which then made unwished-for headlines as the result of a rape – and iT closed down. After the new millennium it started up again, but then the club was raided for drugs, and the party was over for good.

Address Amstelstraat 16, NL-1017 DA Amsterdam (Centrum) | Getting there Metro 51, 53 or 54 to Waterlooplein | Hours Thu & Sun 11.30pm–4am, Fri & Sat 11pm–5am | Tip Cooldown Café round the corner on Rembrandtplein is a place to finish up in the evening – or early morning.

3__ The Amsterdamse Bos
The city's green lung

Apart from a certain plant with its somewhat distinctive leaves, Amsterdam is not necessarily thought of as a green city. Grey stone and red brick predominate. Vondel Park is the biggest in the city, with a not particularly impressive size of 45 hectares (by comparison: Hyde Park in London covers 142 hectares, Central Park in New York 315 hectares). Almost 100 years ago, the mayor of Amsterdam suggested to the head of neighbouring Amstelveen that they should create a park jointly.

As we are still aware today, big projects tend to drag on. In 1934, when work finally commenced, the Great Depression had broken out, and laying out an area for recreation became a major job creation scheme for the unemployed of the city. The work was completed after World War II, but the last tree was not planted until as late as 1970.

The Amsterdamse Bos was conceived as a mixture of German and English park design. However, as some trees have now reached a ripe old age, in places it almost looks like mature woodland. The facilities also include a small stage in the woods, a camp site, a pancake restaurant and a beach for nude bathing. Rowers – high-performance athletes as well as amateurs – can compete on the Bosbaan. Leisure sports are also catered for: horse riding, canoeing, sledging in winter – a full programme of recreation.

Local residents quickly took to the Amsterdamse Bos and made it their green oasis. In the hippie years, concerts were held here. Just as at Woodstock, their great role model, they struggled against rain, mud and an inadequate power supply. Later, demonstrations against the Vietnam War took place here.

Today, the people of Amsterdam use this green area as follows: 26 per cent go walking, 20 per cent exercise their dogs, 20 per cent are joggers, 14 per cent enjoy the natural environment, 12 per cent go to the restaurant, and 10 per cent ride their bikes.

Address Bosbaanweg 5, NL-1182 DA Amstelveen | **Getting there** From Centraal Station bus 170, 172 to Koenenkade; by car: on the A 10 (ring road) to the Buitenveldert exit (S 108), then out of the city on Amstelveenseweg; Bosbaan is the first big crossroads on the right. | **Hours** Accessible 24 hours | **Tip** The Fun Forest, right at the entrance to the woods, is a climbing adventure for children taller than 130 centimetres.

4 The André Hazes Monument

H6 enjoyed life to the full

Those who are old enough might be able to remember the many strange acts that were once exported from Holland (Pussycat with 'Mississiiiiiiiiiiipi', George Baker Selection, Vader Abraham and others). Of course, there were also some good acts, and the current presence of the Dutch in the field of electronic dance music (Tiësto, Fedde Le Grand, Armin van Buuren and so on), for example, is impressive. It must be connected to the party mood of their compatriots.

Alongside this there is also a genre of so-called folk music. Here it is difficult to know whether it is regrettable or a stroke of luck that the music is practically unknown beyond the borders of the Netherlands. One of its more prominent representatives was André Hazes, whose surname was abbreviated by fans to 'H6' (6 in Dutch is 'zes'). Hazes grew up in Amsterdam's De Pijp district, and his talent for singing was discovered at the age of eight when he belted out songs on Albert Cuyp Market. His trademark pieces were big ballads, rendered ardently with lots of feeling and vibrato. Although the ballads were often more reminiscent of chants than of songs with clear melodic lines, large audiences joined in enthusiastically. Most fans almost knew the songs better than the singer himself did. Yet when André was a little boy, he wanted to play rock 'n' roll or rhythm and blues.

Hazes, whose considerable thirst did not extend to a passion for milk, died on 23 September, 2004. Posthumously his song *Zij gelooft in mij* (She Believes in Me) was re-released and became his biggest hit. Almost 50,000 of his followers said farewell in the Amsterdam ArenA. A year later, some of his ashes were scattered over the sea from the beach of Hoek van Holland, and on the same day a monument to Hazes was unveiled on the marketplace in Albert Cuypstraat – on the very spot where his eventful career began.

Address Albert Cuypstraat, NL-1072 CN Amsterdam (Zuid/De Pijp) | Getting there Tram 16 or 24 to Albert Cuypstraat | Tip Caffe 500 (Albert Cuypstraat 59) is an entertaining place with a genuine Fiat 500 as part of its interior furnishings. And the espresso is excellent, too.

5 The Anne Frank Monument

Flight to a foreign country

When Anne Frank moved from Frankfurt to the Dutch capital with her family in 1934, they were refugees, and had to start a new life from scratch. Her father, Otto Frank, succeeded quickly in establishing a position in the Dutch business world. They moved to Merwedeplein, then a newly built area, bright, airy and modern. Anne Frank spent the happiest years of her life here. This period lasted until the German occupation in May 1940. In order to escape deportation to Auschwitz, from 1942 the Franks lived in a house at the back of the company premises of Anne's father in Prinsengracht. Here Anne started to keep her diary, which later became world-famous. On 4 August, 1944 Anne Frank and the seven others who were in hiding there were discovered and arrested. They were taken to the camp at Westerbork, and from there to Auschwitz. Anne Frank died in March 1945 in the Bergen-Belsen concentration camp, probably of typhus and the effects of camp life.

A few years ago, a Dutch television channel hit upon the idea of holding a vote to decide who were the most famous people from the Netherlands. Among the candidates was Anne Frank. In the course of this it was noticed that she had never acquired Dutch nationality. She was deprived of her German nationality in 1941, and after that was a stateless person. Following this discovery, an attempt was made to give Dutch citizenship posthumously to Anne Frank, but bureaucratic obstacles prevented this: according to the laws on naturalisation, citizenship can only be conferred on living persons. Anne Frank's name was put forward nevertheless for the television vote, and she was awarded eighth place.

The monument on Merwedeplein was unveiled on 9 July, 2005. Anne Frank is the only person from Amsterdam who has been honoured with the inauguration of two memorials. The other one stands close to the Westerkerk.

Address Merwedeplein, NL-1078 Amsterdam (Rivierenbuurt) | Getting there Tram 12 or 25 to Waalstraat | Tip Visit the Anne Frank House at Prinsengracht 263. Don't be put off by the fact that names like Justin Bieber can be found in the guest book.

6_ De Appel
A golden apple for artists

The Gouden Eeuw – the Dutch Golden Age, the 17th century – saw an unprecedented flourishing of the art of painting. Merchants in the prosperous cities got rich quickly and wanted to show their wealth. This demand was met by countless still-lifes with their love of detail and portraits of well-fed merchant families looking out at the world in a self-satisfied manner. Not to forget the works of Rembrandt (a name that you will encounter again and again in this book).

But even after the golden century, further painters became world-famous – Van Gogh and Mondrian, for example. Which gives rise to the question: what is happening in our times?

If you want to know the answer to this question, take a look inside De Appel, a centre for contemporary art. It was founded in 1975, at that time in different premises, in a house on a canal that had once belonged to a merchant called Appel. De Appel has a two-fold strategy. On the one hand, of course it gives up-and-coming artists the opportunity to present their works to the public. This is flanked by the usual events and performances. On the other hand, efforts are also made to improve the knowledge of both the public and the young curators. Gallery owners, too, can learn something here. In view of the fact that even open-minded people react to some forms of modern culture in a way that is, shall we say, uncomprehending, this seems to be a good idea.

De Appel is not only a mover and shaker in the city – it has also moved itself. For a long time, the art centre occupied a building named Fantasio, once a rock palace where bands including Led Zeppelin and Pink Floyd took the stage.

In spring 2017, De Appel moved out to the Nieuw West district. In doing so, it is pursuing the 'broedplaats' (breeding ground) strategy: to bring life to less attractive districts by establishing breeding grounds for creativity.

Address Schipluidenlaan 12, NL-1062 HE Amsterdam (West) | Getting there Tram 1, 17 to Cornelis Lelylaan | Hours Variable; it is best to check at www.deappel.nl | Tip The Volkshotel at Wibautstraat 150 is another cradle for art, where you can also have a party and stay overnight.

7___Artis

A perfect paradise for animals

Amsterdam Zoo recently celebrated its 175th anniversary. It was founded in 1838 by a society that had the motto 'Natura Artis Magistra' (which means, as everyone knows who had to learn a bit of Latin at school, 'I came, I saw, I conquered.'[1]), and the Amsterdamers abbreviated this to Artis.

Artis is a typical city zoo dating from the 19th century. That means it has a lot of historic buildings, which may be nice to look at, but on the other hand drive animal conservationists crazy, because in the last-but-one century their ideas about suitable conditions for keeping animals were different from the way we think today. The second problem is the restricted space resulting from an urban location. Artis has been extended and rebuilt time and again. When it first opened, the canal that passes through the zoo was still used for commercial shipping. This annoyed the zoo staff, as boatmen who came through at night sometimes secretly took along passengers, who could then look around the zoo without paying admission.

Artis survived the years of German occupation with relatively little damage. Its director at that time came from Switzerland, and he had learned how to be neutral and stay out of trouble.

Like other zoos, Artis has a mascot and a cute baby animal, an elephant called Mumba. Now you may well ask: why should I visit a zoo in Amsterdam that has the same things as the one where I live? There are two reasons to go: first, a trip to Artis takes you out beyond the belt of canals, and that is basically a good thing. Second, in the zoo aquarium there is a model of Amsterdam's canals. Here you can see something that is not visible anywhere else: how things look below the surface of the water. This is truly astonishing: you would hardly believe what some people throw in a canal.

[1] Only joking! The correct version is 'Nature is the teacher of art'.

Address Plantage Kerklaan 40, NL-1018 CZ Amsterdam (Weesperbuurt) | Getting there
Tram 9 or 14 to Plantage Kerklaan | Hours Apr–Oct 9am–6pm; Nov–Mar 9am–5pm | Tip
The Tropical Museum (Linnaeusstraat 2) has an exotic collection that was once in Artis.

8 Asscher Diamond Cutters
The cut of his life

The Royal Asscher Diamond Company has been family-owned for generations, but is closed to public gaze – no tours of the premises are on offer. Yet this is an interesting place, as here, quite literally, cutting-edge techniques were developed.

This expertise was used to cut the Cullinan, the world's largest diamond, which was found in South Africa on 26 January, 1905. The raw diamond, a 3,106-carat stone, weighed over half a kilo.

The Cullinan was delivered by registered parcel post to King Edward VII of England, while an imitation stone was sent to London under guard to mislead potential thieves. As for the imitation, Inspector Clouseau … but no, that's another story.

The head of the company, Joseph Asscher, personally attended to the cutting and polishing of the Cullinan. He was considered the world's best diamond cutter. Before he undertook the task, he incised a small 'window' into the diamond, as a means of understanding better where its fault lines lay. After that, he went around for days with the diamond in his pocket, feeling it again and again until his sense of touch had made him familiar with its structure.

On 10 February, 1908 he was ready. Joseph Asscher made a small incision in the diamond in preparation for the work. If he had made a mistake at this stage, the stone would have shattered into a thousand fragments like the safety glass in a modern car windscreen. Asscher was so tense when he made the first cut that he fainted. Nevertheless, his technique was flawless.

The Cullinan was made into nine large and 96 smaller diamonds. The largest of them, 530.2 carats, called the Great Star of Africa, was set into the sovereign's sceptre and cross, part of the Crown Jewels, but can also be removed and worn as a brooch. A smaller Cullinan stone, the Lesser Star of Africa, was shown by the Queen in 1958 to Louis, brother of Joseph Asscher.

Address Tolstraat 127, NL-1074 VJ Amsterdam (Zuid / De Pijp) | Getting there Tram 4 to Lutmastraat | Tip Take a look at the cottages in this area, built by Gerard Adriaan Heineken, founder of the Heineken brewery, for his workers.

9 __ The Aviodrome

For flying Dutchmen

Anthony Fokker, born in 1890, was Holland's pioneer of flight, the Dutch answer to the Wright brothers. When he went to Germany in 1910 to train as a technician, he had already made up his mind that his future career would be devoted to flying. Fokker was an all-rounder: a developer, engineer, businessman and test pilot for his own aircraft.

In those days there was still an aerodrome in the district of Johannisthal in Berlin. The first aircraft builders had set up shop around this airstrip. Fokker, too, built his plant here and designed the Fokker triplane. Production was later moved to Schwerin in the province of Mecklenburg, where Fokker developed further models in which the famous 'Red Baron', Manfred von Richthofen, flew in combat with such success in World War I. It was an invention by Fokker that gave the German flying machines an advantage in the first years of the war. He synchronised the plane's machine guns and propeller so that the pilots could fire ahead of them without damaging their own propeller blades. After the war, he returned to his home in the Netherlands, where he founded a new aircraft company.

The Fokker brand no longer produces aircraft, even though there are still planes in the air that bear this name. The Dutch airline KLM, once a proud national carrier, merged with Air France long ago. Nevertheless, to gain an impression of the importance of the history of air travel in the Netherlands, it is well worth paying a visit to the Aviodrome in Lelystad, about one hour by car from Amsterdam. Here you can learn about almost 200 years of the history of human flight. There is an aircraft simulator, a jumbo jet that visitors can view from inside and a reconstruction of the reception building of Schiphol Airport in 1928. If you would like to take to the air yourself, it is possible to book a round trip in a plane.

Address Aviodrome Lelystad, Pelikaanweg 50, NL-8218 PG Lelystad | **Getting there** From Centraal Station intercity trains go every half hour or more often to Lelystad; by car: from Amsterdam via the A1 and A6 to Lelystad, Luchthaven exit, then take Larserweg (N302) about 1 km in the direction of Harderwijk | **Hours** Tue–Sun 10am–5pm; further information at www.aviodrome.nl | **Tip** If you don't like to travel at altitude, stay at sea level and take a jetfoil from the harbour of Amsterdam to IJmuiden.

10 The Avontuur
Hoist the sails

The Dutch language is full of expressions that derive from sailing. As in English, where there are phrases like 'don't go overboard', 'take the wind out of his sails', 'I don't like the cut of his jib' and 'shipshape and Bristol fashion', the Dutch have many sailors' sayings and turns of phrase that have entered the general language and can be applied to every aspect of daily life.

This is natural in a country that is historically one of the great maritime nations, which grew rich in its Golden Age, the 17th century, from trading in European waters and all across the globe, and where everybody lived close to the coast or to a river or canal that was an important means of transport.

Taking pride in the victories of the Royal Navy, the English are apt to forget that its greatest disaster was in 1667, when the Dutch fleet raided the river Medway and destroyed 15 English warships. In past centuries, the handling of a sailing boat was as natural to people in the Netherlands as riding a bicycle today.

But back to the present day. The Avontuur, a clipper launched in 1909, is available to everyone who is interested in a sailing trip, for getting seasick, taking part in a race, or even hiring for a long expedition.

A clipper is actually an anachronism: when they were built, steamships were already common, but on certain routes clippers, usually with a steel hull and a huge area of sail, were still superior to their modern competitors. They were given the name 'clipper' on account of their speed, as they flitted across the oceans at a fast clip, as if they were cutting (clipping) through wind and water.

Avontuur is not one of the really big clippers, but large enough to convey an active impression of the era when the Netherlands was a great maritime power. To ensure that the vessel is never becalmed, there is also an engine on board for every eventuality.

Address Van Diemenkade 14, NL-1013 CR Amsterdam (Centrum) | Getting there
Tram 3 to Zoutkeetsgracht | Hours Bookings and information: www.avontuur.nl
or +31 (6)14045800 | Tip If you want to start small and do the sailing yourself, at the
Nautiek sailing school (Veemkade 267) you can hire a dinghy on a lake.

11 The Bar Americain
Water and wine, beer and ballads

What do Americans do when they are abroad? Rick (Humphrey Bogart), the famous American expat from the film *Casablanca*, set up his Café Américain. There is one of these establishments in Amsterdam too, and a bar to match next door. It comes as no surprise that Americans on their travels come here, and if anyone among them is better-known than the others, he or she is honoured with a photo on the wall.

Here is just a small selection of the English speakers (not only Americans, but British and Canadians too, as well as a few from Ireland, even if they are not entirely happy with the context), in strict alphabetical order of their first names: Amy Winehouse, Bill Wyman, Billy Gibbons (ZZ Top), Bruce Springsteen, Cindy Lauper, Cliff Richard, Dusty Hill (ZZ Top), Eric Clapton, the Everly Brothers, Frank Beard (ZZ Top), Gloria Estefan, Jamie Cullum, Jeff Healey, Joe Cocker, John Forsythe, Johnny Logan, Jon Bon Jovi, Lenny Kravitz, Leonard Cohen, Liam Gallagher (Oasis), Mick Hucknall (Simply Red), Noel Gallagher (Oasis), Robert Plant, Seal, Sean Lennon, Willy DeVille, Willy Nelson and so on and so on.

The list could be extended much further. It is generally believed that the young Robbie Williams came here for some Dutch courage on his first visit to the city before getting his first tattoo from Henk Schiffmacher (see ch. 86). It is said to have been a Celtic cross.

With all these celebrity guests from the music business, it is inevitable that something like a spontaneous jam session develops late in the evening. The barkeepers were, and are, quite happy about that. Things get a little more difficult when people who have not been blessed by nature with huge talent suddenly want to tinkle the ivories and start to sing. As many a barman knows from his own painful experience: 'After a few drinks, a lot of people think they are great artists'.

Address Leidsekade 97, NL-1017 PN Amsterdam (Centrum) | **Getting there** Tram 1, 2 or 5 to Leidseplein | **Hours** Daily 5pm–1am | **Tip** In the Xtra Cold Icebar (Amstel 194–196) everything is ice-cold: the drinks, the fittings and the room temperature. It's the place to go if you are extremely cool.

12__Battello

Gondolas in the Venice of the North

For centuries Amsterdam has been described as the 'Venice of the North' – a logical comparison in view of the numerous canals that criss-cross the city. Of course, these small canals have been used since time immemorial as arteries of transport and for pleasure trips. But it was a long time before it occurred to anyone to put a typical Venetian gondola on the water in Amsterdam.

Then Tirza Mol and Leentje Visser had their idea for founding a company. These two women had both studied boat building, and as part of their final dissertation made a functioning replica of an Italian gondola. The vessel is 11 metres long, painted the traditional black and – something that is too readily forgotten among all the jokes and cartoons that feature gondolas and gondolieri – is also not at all easy to steer. After all, a gondoliere has no more than a single oar, which is attached to one side of the boat and in principle only amounts to a long pole with a wooden board at the bottom.

Wishing to learn to perfect the art of navigating a gondola, the two boat builders set off for Venice to learn the skill from local experts, working at the Tramontin yard.

This was not simple, as the art of handling a gondola is restricted in Venice to a secretive guild in which the requisite knowledge is passed down from generation to generation. Every trick and skill is handed on from father to son. When a woman arrives from the north of Europe who doesn't want to lie back and listen to an aria, but really wants to understand how it is done, she encounters scepticism and rejection at first. However, the budding gondolieri from Amsterdam eventually found masters of the craft who initiated them into the secrets.

Today, Stichting Battello in Amsterdam operates round trips on the canals. If you should book one, and feel a desire to belt out *O Sole Mio* – it's better to forget the idea.

Address Herenmarkt pier, NL-1013 ED Amsterdam (Centrum) | **Getting there**
Bus 18, 21, 22, 348 or 353 to Singel | **Hours** Trips by arrangement: +31 (20)6869868,
www.gondel.nl | **Tip** Even more exotic is a trip with a tuk-tuk, a cross between a moped
and a rickshaw (www.tuktukuitjes.nl/index.php).

13 De Bijenkorf

Big business, busy as a bee

The department store De Bijenkorf ('the bee hive') is part of a chain of such stores, with branches in other Dutch cities. De Bijenkorf in Amsterdam is the largest of them, with a sales area of 20,000 square metres, and claims in its advertising to be the largest and most exclusive department store in the city. It likes to see itself as being in the same league as Harrods in London, Galeries Lafayette in Paris and KaDeWe in Berlin. This is reasonable as far as the range of goods and the atmosphere are concerned, but not necessarily in terms of location – but more of that later.

Today, this bee hive belongs to an Anglo-Canadian investment group, but it started out in the late 19th century, when big department stores emerged in other countries, too. Its founder, Simon Philip Goudsmit, set up in business in 1870 with a haberdashery shop at Nieuwendijk 132. The foundation stone for today's building was laid in 1909. De Bijenkorf was a trendsetter in many ways: the first escalator in Holland was installed here, for example. The building is also a TV star. Nearby on Dam, the memorial ceremony for the fallen of World War II takes place every year in early May, and is broadcast on television. It is fitting that the store should be the backdrop, as 700 members of its staff lost their lives during the German occupation.

Whether it is worth going to Amsterdam for the shopping is doubtful. Since the introduction of the euro, the city has ceased to be attractive for bargain hunters from neighbouring countries, as the price tags in the store confirm. However, the atmosphere there is unique, not least because De Bijenkorf is situated at the apex of an equilateral triangle, right between the red-light district and the exchange. This location alone can teach more about how human beings get along together than a university semester in Sociology.

Address Dam 1, NL-1012 JS Amsterdam (Centrum) | Getting there Tram 4, 9, 16, 24, 25 or 26 to Dam | Hours Mon 11am–8pm, Tue & Wed 10am–8pm, Thu & Fri 10am–9pm, Sat 9.30am–8pm, Sun 11am–8pm | Tip If shopping interests you less than watching the local celebrities, or people who think they are celebrities, shopping, go to Peter Cornelisz Hooftstraat (close to the Museum Quarter).

14 The Bijlmer Experience

A mystery on the edge of the city

Bijlmer is a district in the south-east of Amsterdam, a part of the city into which tourists seldom stray. Many people think there is not much to see there. A sea of concrete housing blocks, social conflicts, groups at the margins of society. There are many here who feel excluded and deprived of opportunities. You might think it is a problematic district like many others. Yet Bijlmer is world-famous – at least among conspiracy theorists.

On 4 October, 1992 a jumbo jet of the Israeli airline El Al crashed onto the Groeneveen and Klein-Kruitberg residential blocks. The official casualties of the crash were 43 people, including the plane's crew of three and one passenger, who has not been identified to this day. Other sources suspect that the number of fatalities was higher, because in the housing estates there may have been illegal immigrants who were not registered. After the crash, looting took place that was finally ended by mounted police.

The aircraft was on the way from New York to Tel Aviv and had put in a stop at Amsterdam's Schiphol Airport. The cause of the crash was clearly that the plane lost two of its engines shortly after taking off.

This alone was highly unusual, but even more controversy surrounded the question of the freight that was on board. The arrival of dozens of men at the site of the disaster shortly after it happened, who examined the wreckage wearing white protective suits, fuelled speculation further. There were rumours of a secret military cargo. Soon local residents were complaining of health problems. Political investigations followed, but failed to settle all the open questions.

Those who would like to know more – and are also open to the idea that there are truly some interesting things to discover in this district – should take a look at the Bijlmer Experience, which is a cross between a guided tour and an exhibition.

Address Nellesteinpad, NL-1103 Amsterdam (Zuidoost) | Getting there Metro 53 to
Kraaiennest | Hours Tours by arrangement: +31 (6)24856709 or www.ilovezuidoost.nl |
Tip Brussels has the *Manneken Pis*, but Bijlmer has a sculpture called *Tayouken Piss*
(*Les Pisseurs d'Amsterdam*). Faster, higher, stronger.

15 The Blauwbrug

A black day on the Blue Bridge

Officially, the bridge is known as number 236. It spans the river Amstel and connects Amstelstraat with Waterlooplein. The usual name of the bridge derives from its predecessor rather than from the blue lamps that pay homage to its heritage.

This is the only bridge in Amsterdam whose design was modelled on those in Paris. This alone ought to earn the Blue Bridge a mention in some of the travel guides and books about the city, but in fact it became famous for a different reason – the events on a specific date.

On 30 April, 1980 Queen Juliana abdicated and passed on the throne to her daughter Beatrix and husband Claus. It is easier to understand all the fuss and excitement at the coronation of Beatrix's successor, King Willem-Alexander and his consort Máxima, and also the joy at the harmonious manner of their succession, if you call to mind the events a generation earlier.

Holland was gripped by an economic crisis. As in other European cities, there was a squatter scene of militants in occupied houses, who at best felt that their needs were not understood by politicians, and in extreme cases felt threatened. The atmosphere was explosive. In advance of a demonstration that was scheduled to take place on the same day as the coronation of Beatrix, flyers were passed around the city calling on demonstrators to wear a helmet. It was feared that the situation might escalate into something like civil war.

The police resorted to water cannon and truncheons. Some of them, dressed in civilian clothes, mixed with the demonstrators to track down the ringleaders. The fighting began in the morning in Bilderdijkstraat and came to a climax on the Blue Bridge, eventually ending on Leidseplein. At times it really did seem that a civil war was in progress. To this day, 30 April, 1980 is regarded as the most violent day in the Netherlands since World War II.

Address Waterlooplein, NL-1011 PG Amsterdam (Centrum) | Getting there Metro 51, 53 or 54 to Waterlooplein | Tip If you are interested in monarchy, make the trip to Doorn to visit the house where the last German emperor, Kaiser Wilhelm II, spent the final years of his life in exile.

16 __ The Blijburg

A roaming beach

The fact that you see words in Holland such as 'het IJ', IJburg or IJmuiden is not caused by the fact that the Dutch have fat fingers, so on a keyboard they always hit two letters at once. The reason is that IJ is a distinct sound that has its own place in the alphabet of the telephone directory, between X and Y.

To make the matter even more complicated for foreigners, it was and is sometimes written as 'y', which is why you sometimes read the name 'Cruijff', but sometimes alternatively 'Cruyff'. The pronunciation of this diphthong is as difficult for many foreigners as saying a 'th' in English, though not such a tough challenge as the Dutch 'ui'. You will possibly get closest to the pronunciation of a Dutch IJ if you imagine an unsophisticated character from a scripted-reality television series for afternoon viewing. Something like: 'Eyyyy, you stupid cow, what's wrong with you?!'

Having practised this, you can now venture on a journey to IJburg, during which you will hear that it is a man-made island in a body of water in Amsterdam called the IJ. This land was reclaimed to create space for housing as the city sprawled out to the south-east.

As the city keeps on expanding, it pushes the beach resort called Blijburg (meaning, roughly, Blissburg) further and further out. Blijburg 1.0 was opened in 2003 on the Haveneiland, but closed again by autumn 2005, as the construction of housing had meanwhile made more progress. The beach, too, which has a rather bohemian air, moved on, but opened up again a few years later. This process has been repeated for some time now, and in the meantime the beach's disposition to roam has become its trademark. Of course, if you want a trip out to the seaside, you could travel a little further to Zandvoort. On the other hand, the idea of a beach that keeps moving on and always stays in contact with the city has a charm all of its own.

Address Muiderlaan 1001, NL-1087 VA Amsterdam (Oost) | Getting there Bus 66 to IJburg Strand | Hours Mon–Fri from 11am, Sat & Sun from 10am; if the weather is bad, phone +31 (20)4160330 | Tip If you would like to camp like the Dutch in Amsterdam, you can do it in Zeeburg (www.campingzeeburg.nl.).

17__Bureau Warmoesstraat

Morality and sin in the heart of the city

The police station in Warmoesstraat is well known in Amsterdam. Many stories and myths surround it. At least one police commissar who served here for a long time became a legendary figure after telling of his experiences in a book. The ingredients and the gallery of characters who feature in their tales were not, however, particularly surprising.

They shocked the reading public with stories of brutal murders and other acts of cruelty, of prostitutes with a heart of gold and knowledge of life – and, among all of this, policemen marked by their experiences, who had seen everything human life had to offer and whose wisdom and far-sightedness ensured that this quarter of the city remained part of the civilised world and did not descend into conditions like those in Sodom and Gomorrah.

If the reminiscences of retired cops seem to be greatly idealised, the world of fiction painted events in even more lurid colours. The most successful author was Appie Baantjer, who was a policeman himself before he took up writing. The detective he created, De Cock, treads slowly through his district like a reborn Maigret. He is supported by a team of assistants who are all younger and quicker, but who would be at a loss without the wisdom of the old policeman.

Many of these novels were made into films. There are some exciting and moving moments in the stories, but they are not quite like Peter Falk playing Inspector Columbo, and sometimes viewers get the feeling that they are watching paint dry or grass grow – though this is something that, out of politeness, you should never say to the Dutch. The series is extremely popular in the Netherlands, and a visit to the police station, called Bureau Warmoesstraat, is without doubt interesting: here you can visit a place in which comforting myths were woven from the threads of a reality that was often depressing.

Address Warmoesstraat 66, NL-1012 JH Amsterdam (Centrum) | Getting there Tram 4, 9, 16, 24, 25 or 26 to Dam | Hours Mon 10am–1pm; Van Aemstel Produkties (+31 (20)6832592) runs interesting guided tours. | Tip Another former police station, at Buiksloterweg 9b, is a place of architectural interest.

18__Café Brecht

A home for urban poets

Given Dutch attitudes to Germany, some people may be surprised, and others not, to learn that in Amsterdam, Berlin has been regarded as a cool city for a few years now. The result of this is that a variety of events, whether high culture or pop culture, have German names and locations are declared to be 'typical of Berlin'.

Whether these claims are accurate is often a matter for debate, but not in the case of Café Brecht. Its owner, Joris Houtman, spent a good deal of time in Berlin, and when he returned to his home town he missed the kind of pub that he had learned to appreciate in the trendy districts of the German capital: a bit like a living room filled with heavy, elaborate furniture, old standard lamps, armchairs, and settees from grandfather's day. 'Cheap chic' was his name for this style. So he fitted out a place in this fashion. The style is popular with his customers, who are mostly but not all students. The pub is usually full, and in the evening it can get really lively.

On the walls are portraits of Marlene Dietrich and other German artists from the era of the Weimar Republic. The programme organisers regard Café Brecht as a haven of European culture, and stick to their principles consistently. Alongside lieder by Kurt Weill and Lotte Lenya, you can hear French or Belgian chansons and Italian songs. The drinks menu, too, is strictly continental – tequila is nowhere to be found.

Through the influence of his parents, Joris became familiar with German writers at an early age, as they listened to audio books of works by Erich Kästner and Heinrich Böll during car journeys – at a time when many Dutch people, when Germany was mentioned, could think of nothing more than the world wars and football. The result is that Café Brecht puts on an ambitious and entertaining programme, often with German literature, but not everything is highbrow.

Address Weteringschans 157, NL-1017 SE Amsterdam (Centrum) | Getting there Tram 12, 16 or 25 to Weteringscircuit | **Hours** Daily noon–1am, programme details at www.cafebrecht.nl | **Tip** Another place that advertises its 'Berlin atmosphere' is De Nieuwe Anita at Frederik Hendrikstraat 111.

19 Café 't Mandje

Bet the biker, a pioneer

Holland in general – and Amsterdam in particular – has long been regarded as a haven of tolerance, including sexual tolerance. Clichés, whether favourable or not, often have a basis in truth, but are also liable to exaggeration. In Amsterdam, as elsewhere, attacks on minority groups take place, but this does not alter the fact that the city is one of the world's more tolerant places. But it was necessary to fight for this virtue.

Bet van Beeren was a real Amsterdam character. She was born in Jordaan at the start of the 20th century at a time when this district was still regarded as the purest essence of the Amsterdam way of life. In 1927, when she was just 25 years old, she opened Café 't Mandje on Zeedijk. This was a notorious area in those days, but Bet had little difficulty in holding her own. She drank hard liquor like water, cursed and swore, and wore heavy leather gear when she rode her motorbike – and now it should not surprise anyone that she made no secret of being a lesbian.

Under German occupation she continued to run her café, and gave shelter to persecuted Jews. After the war, Mandje was the first café that welcomed homosexuals. This broke a spell, as until then there had only been clubs with restricted admission, which operated every bit as secretly as the undercover Catholic churches after the Netherlands broke away from Spanish rule.

In Amsterdam Bet van Beeren is still seen as a local hero, but she was denied wider recognition in society. When the later Queen Beatrix demonstratively paid a visit to the red-light district in 1965, Bet's establishment was ignored. She was greatly offended by this. Two years later, she died – of liver disease, fittingly for a pub landlady. After her demise, Café 't Mandje closed down. Recently it has reopened, and is now run by her niece Diana along lines of which Bet would have approved.

Address Zeedijk 63, NL-1012 AS Amsterdam (Centrum) | **Getting there** Metro 51, 53, 54 to Nieuwmarkt | **Hours** Tue & Wed 4pm–1am, Thu 3pm–1am, Fri & Sat 2pm–3am, Sun 2pm–1am; further information at www.cafetmandje.nl | **Tip** The homosexual monument on Westermarkt was unveiled in 1987. It is the first of its kind worldwide.

20___Café Papeneiland

Cake for Clinton, recipes for Hillary

Café Papeneiland has been owned for generations by a family in which experience of how to run a place to eat and drink has been passed on reliably from father to son and from mother to daughter. This is impressive, but not, as an attentive reader of these pages will have realised, unique in Amsterdam.

The history of Café Papeneiland goes back a very long way. It has been in existence since 1642, and has protected heritage status, of course. Since its foundation, it has had an escape route for ministers of religion whose beliefs differed from the established denomination of the country. This escape route has survived, and the café took its name from the fleeing priests, 'papen'.

This is interesting and all very well, but does not necessarily make the café unique. There are older ones, for example Karpershoek (see ch. 52). But we have not finished yet. Café Papeneiland is situated at the point where two canals meet. At the water's edge there is a jetty, enabling guests to arrive by boat. Anyone who wants to explore Jordaan from here on foot or by bike can get advice at the counter, including a map of the district and tips about where to hire a bike at a reasonable price.

This too is a pleasant characteristic, but what distinguishes this café from all the others is its celebrated clientele. In 2011 the former US president Clinton was a guest here. He ate some apple cake and took the opportunity to show he has the common touch. Before taking his leave, he bought a whole apple cake for Hillary (or did he eat some of it himself?) and sent a letter of thanks. This has now been framed and hung behind the counter between newspaper cuttings and other curiosities from the long, eventful history of the building. But don't be put off by this visit from an international celebrity: Café Papeneiland is extremely cosy and very typical of Amsterdam.

Address Prinsengracht 2, NL-1015 DV Amsterdam (Centrum) | Getting there Bus 18, 21, 22 or 353 to Buiten Brouwersstraat | Hours Mon–Thu & Sun 11–1am, Sat 11–2am | Tip Another well-known, though not world-famous patisserie is Kwekkeboom, for example at Reguliersbreestraat 36.

21 Café-Restaurant 1e Klas
First-class service for all

It is absolutely clear to me that you can be suspected of laziness if you praise as a 'must-see', a café situated in the central station. Is somebody trying to avoid setting off to explore? Don't jump to conclusions. There are excellent arguments for featuring this establishment. Of course, there are various unusual cafés and restaurants elsewhere in Amsterdam, but more than a few of them have a strange deficiency.

The Dutch are the tallest people in Europe – not only in terms of the statistical average, but based on the empirical evidence of a walk around the city. You have the impression that most of the locals whom you encounter are tall.

And there is one thing that your author has never understood: why do Amsterdamers favour cafés where the chairs are no higher than upturned buckets and the tables as small as milking stools? To be quite frank, this is rarely comfortable, and it also makes things crowded. When your neighbour waves to the waiter and has a pointed elbow, it can be really unpleasant.

One shining exception to this is the café in the central station, with its very imposing Art Nouveau décor that dates back to 1881. It is truly a first-class restaurant, and is furnished with chairs that were not conceived by a designer of dolls' houses and has fittings whose dimensions are suited to what the average western European regards as comfortable and convenient – not to forget the waiters, who exude a dignified and cosmopolitan air that is fitting for the location. All of this is reminiscent of the days of travel, rather than mass transit systems. In a station restaurant, guests mainly spend their time waiting for a train, but in this one it is well worth stopping for a while after arriving in Amsterdam and before immersing yourself in its urban adventure. If you do this, the discomforts that you may encounter later will be easier to bear.

Address Stationsplein 15 (platform 2b, Centraal Station, NL-1012 AB Amsterdam (Centrum) | Getting there Centraal Station | Hours Daily 8.30am–11pm (food until 10pm) | Tip Café De Jaren (Nieuwe Doelenstraat 20–22) is in the same league in terms of the spacious interior and atmosphere.

22__Carré

An arena for the circus and vaudeville

The Carré family (not to be confused with Le Carré) was an old-established dynasty of fairground entertainers with German and French roots that was given permission to build a circus in the 19th century. They moved their base several times before opening the present building in 1887. In the course of time, the programme changed: less circus, more vaudeville. All the big names of the Golden Twenties took the stage here: Josephine Baker performed her dance in a banana skirt, the Comedian Harmonists sang harmoniously, Italian opera and popular theatre were staged.

The 1950s saw the start of the great love of Dutch people for musicals, which continues to this day. In 1957 *Porgy and Bess* was performed, and the first production in Dutch of *My Fair Lady* followed. In 1986 *Cats* arrived, a show with which the Dutch creators of musicals finally reached their goal of world-class quality. This was followed by *West Side Story*, *Fiddler on the Roof*, *Annie* and *Evita* – all of them huge successes.

But by no means everything was traditional. Frank Zappa's musical *200 Motels* had its première here, and a great number of international stars performed at the venue. They were usually people who were not noisy enough for the pop temple Paradiso: James Taylor, Buena Vista Social Club, Stomp, Dave Brubeck, Laura Pausini, Noa, Bette Midler, Oleta Adams, Udo Jürgens, Dulce Pontes, Paolo Conte, Jewel, Georges Moustaki, Van Morrison, Dionne Warwick, Mercedes Sosa, Julien Clerc, Randy Newman, Lou Reed and others. Herman van Veen made his breakthrough as a solo artist here.

Again and again the continued existence of Carré was under threat, and this insecurity did not end until 1977, when the city government took over the building for six million guilders (about 2.7 million euros). Since then the advertising slogan 'Carré – a genuine Amsterdam musical theatre' has been true in every way.

Address Amstel 115–125, NL-1018 EM Amsterdam (Centrum) | Getting there Metro 51, 53 or 54 to Weesperplein | Hours Programme: www.carre.nl/index.html | Tip Oscar Carré was buried in an impressive tomb in the Zorgvlied cemetery (Amsteldijk 273), where other famous Amsterdamers lie.

23__Chinatown

Forget it, Jake, it's Chinatown

The Chinatown in the centre of Amsterdam looks every bit as picturesque as you would imagine it to be. Shops, hairdressers, apothecaries, restaurants, massage parlours, fireworks and dragon dancing at Chinese New Year – everything is colourful, strange-looking and exotic, as it has been for many years. After the Chinatown in London, Amsterdam's is the second-oldest in Europe. The story of its origins is anything but romantic, however.

In summer 1911 there was a seamen's strike in Amsterdam. The shipping lines imported 26 Chinese from England as strike breakers. At first, the unions were hardly concerned about this – what difference could a few of these small men make? In the end, 3,000 of them came – to do the dirty work. At that time, most vessels were steamships, and the Chinese were hired as coal carriers. For the rest of the population they were practically invisible.

During the Great Depression, many seamen were unemployed. The Chinese sailors stranded ashore without work baked peanut biscuits and sold them from door to door. This so-called 'pindaman' was such a success that Chinese from all over Europe came to Amsterdam and copied the business idea.

The first Chinese restaurants opened during World War II. When the era of the great passenger liners came to an end, a further wave of unemployment ensued. Many of the sailors who were made redundant then passed their time in a manner familiar from other parts of the world: by gambling and smoking opium. In the 1970s and 1980s, dealing in heroin became a big business in which Chinese gangs engaged. This marked the perception of the Chinese in Amsterdam in the media. It was not the whole story, however. The fact is that, on the contrary, the Chinese community has always demonstrated its vitality in the face of repeated discrimination and setbacks. Today approximately 10,000 Chinese live in Amsterdam.

Address Between Zeedijk (善德街) and Geldersekade (僑德仕街), NL-1012 Amsterdam (Centrum) | Getting there Metro 51, 53 or 54 to Nieuwmarkt | Tip Sea Palace (Osterdokskade 8) is Europe's first floating restaurant. It serves authentic Chinese food on three floors.

24 _ The Condomerie
Tales and shapes of rubber

There are few historic events for which it is absolutely clear when and where they occurred. For Condomerie, the world's first specialist shop for condoms, this is not the case. On 10 April, 1987 a lively discussion took place in a restaurant in Amsterdam about a new disease that had been known for some years under the name AIDS.

Knowledge of this dreadful disease was limited at that time. Alongside a few facts, there were many wild rumours. It had been established that AIDS could spread via bodily fluids such as blood or sperm, though not through saliva in kissing, and that for the time being condoms were the best method of protection.

Following the previous decades of permissiveness, condoms were considered to be anything but cool, however, quite apart from any cultural or religious reservations. When condoms were sold, this took place with embarrassment in hidden-away corners. Where the use of rubber contraceptives was concerned, there was no kind of information, education – or even fun. But today the shop windows of Condomerie are almost as crowded as those in the nearby Red Light District.

Condomerie opened for business on 1 May, 1987 (too late for the parties on Koninginnedag a day earlier, but never mind), when it had a second part to its name: 'the golden fleece'. The opening was newsworthy in itself, but the fact that the shop was run by two women created considerable added interest. The owners were satisfied with the media coverage. The taboo surrounding condoms seemed to have been broken.

From the very beginning it was important to the managers of the shop that the atmosphere should seem friendly and inviting for all customers, whether men or women. The product range is enormous, including an assortment of erotic accoutrements, and so is the know-how offered to customers here, as all of their pressing questions are answered by the staff.

ondomerie.com

Always keep a
rubber on hand

Please 'Like'
Condomerie on Facebook

ALL YOU NEED is LOVE

Address Warmoesstraat 141, NL-1012 JB Amsterdam (Centrum) | **Getting there** Tram 4, 9,
16, 24, 25 or 26 to Dam | **Hours** Mon – Sat 11am – 6pm, Sun 1 – 5pm | **Tip** Unusual coverings
for the rest of the body are sold at the underwear shop Webers Holland, Kloveniersburgwal 26.

25 Coster Diamonds
Diamonds are a man's best friend

When Spain expelled the Moors and Jews, it sowed the seeds of its own later decline. Among the Jews were many diamond cutters, who took their knowledge and their tools with them. As a result, Antwerp and Amsterdam became the centres of the diamond business. Spain conquered almost all of Latin America and discovered huge silver mines, but was never successful, despite all the exploitation of its colonies, because the specialist know-how for administration and processing of the wealth had been lost.

Moses Elias Coster opened his workshop in Amsterdam in 1840. As its original location was sacrificed for construction of the subway, since 1970 the company premises have been at their present address in the Museum Quarter. Coster was a revolutionary. For centuries the polishing machines had been powered by horses, and Coster was the first in the Netherlands to use a steam engine for the purpose. You would think that, by the nature of the business, diamond polishers would not tend to be sloppy in their work, but even by the standards of his colleagues Coster was a conspicuous perfectionist. His excellent reputation even reached the ears of Queen Victoria of England, who employed him to give a new polish to the Koh-i-Noor.

The story of this diamond is as turbulent as the plots of the *Pink Panther* films, except that a detective as incompetent as Inspector Clouseau would not have had the ghost of a chance. In the 14th century this stone was possessed by an Indian rajah who was determined to keep it because, according to a saying of the time, the owner of the Koh-i-Noor was the most powerful man in the world. In the 18th century it was stolen from his descendants; the gem was taken to Persia, where the British then took possession of it. Today a number of different parties claim to be the rightful owner, which is hardly surprising in view of this eventful history.

Address Paulus Potterstraat 2–8, NL-1071 CS Amsterdam (Zuid/Concertgebouwbuurt) | Getting there Tram 2 or 5 to Hobbemastraat | Hours Daily 9am–5pm; public and private tours are available | Tip Asscher diamond cutters at Tolstraat 127 show how precious stones were produced in the early 20th century.

26___ The Cotton Club
All that jazz – and more

This may sound like a joke, but in Amsterdam there was once a time when drugs were exotic and rare, and – even more surprising – the authorities in Amsterdam blamed infringements of the drugs laws on Germany, from where people cross the border today to get their substances in the Netherlands. The reason was that after World War II, American soldiers on their way home passed on narcotics to the locals – but that was a long time ago, back in the 1940s and 1950s.

The Cotton Club opened in 1940, then under the very ordinary name Café Smit. Things did not get more exciting until after the war, when the daughter of the owners took over. She had a friend who played the trumpet, using the pseudonym Teddy Cotton. Soon the name of the club and its programme had changed.

In the 1950s the Cotton Club was one of the few places where 'negro bands', as they were then called, could perform. The programme attracted fans of jazz: black American soldiers, Dutch citizens from the Antilles and Surinam, and of course artists who wanted to go 'on the road' like Jack Kerouac and the beat poets, which was not so easy in a relatively small country like Holland, as the roads were not really long enough. The Cotton Club became famous for its music and infamous for the powerful smell of drugs, and its decline came in the 1970s. Rival gangs made the district a dangerous place. A ship was even sunk once during one of their fights. The quarter went into decline. It used to be said in those days: if you'd rather not have your car windscreen broken by thieves who are after your radio, then it's best to give it to them when you get out.

Nevertheless, the district made a recovery, and so did the Cotton Club. Unwanted guests were driven away with songs by André Hazes (see ch. 4) and operetta, and now good live music is played there again. Jazz, of course – what else?

Address Nieuwmarkt 5, NL-1011 JP Amsterdam (Centrum) | Getting there Metro 51, 53 or 54 to Nieuwmarkt | Hours Mon–Thu 3pm–1am, Fri 11–3am, Sat 10–3am | Tip The North Sea Jazz Club at Pazzanistraat 1 has treats for the ears and the palate: three-course menus including a concert.

27__The Doelen Hotel

The home of the nightwatchmen

This is the site of the building that was supposed to be occupied by the men depicted on Rembrandt's painting *The Night Watch*. The course of the city wall and fortifications was here, and the tower built on this spot was called Swych Utrecht (which means, roughly translated, 'Shut your mouth, Utrecht'). What the people of Utrecht could expect if they ignored this advice is shown by Rembrandt's painting. Its official title, by the way, is *The Company of Captain Frans Banning Cocq and Lieutenant Willem van Ruytenburch Prepares to March* – perhaps not such a catchy title as *The Night Watch*, but when the civic militia commissioned the work, it expected the names of its two commanders to be included.

The work has been interpreted countless times since it was painted, sometimes by people who enjoyed doing so, but possibly more often by people whose duty it was and who had long ago ceased to find any pleasure in art. (And in case you have an explanation of why a little girl is running across the picture, please don't say a word. I want to find out for myself.)

There is one thing that not many people know: Rembrandt – or Rembrandt Harmenszoon van Rijn, as we connoisseurs of art call him – originally did not want to be a painter. On the contrary, he dreamed of a career as a ballet dancer in the ensemble of the East India Company. In his youth he must have spent thousands of hours pirouetting on a bar in front of the mirror, until he turned his ankle, was forced to spend weeks in bed, and started to draw as a result of boredom. Because he was limping about as he drew, he knocked over the candle a number of times, which is the explanation for the light-and-shadow effects that later became legendary in his paintings.[2]

[2] This theory has admittedly not been confirmed one hundred per cent. It is, however, a fact that the Beatles once stayed in the hotel that now stands here.

Address Nieuwe Doelenstraat 24, NL-1012 CP Amsterdam (Centrum) | **Getting there** Tram 4, 9, 16, 24 or 25 to Muntplein | **Hours** The hotel provides normal accommodation, but at www.denachtwacht-themakingof.nl you can book interesting guided tours about the people in the painting and the background to it. | **Tip** To find out more about the life and work of the artist, visit the Rembrandthuis in Jodenbreestraat.

28 __ De Dokter

A Grolsch a day keeps the doctor away

The Dutch love to add a diminutive to the end of a word. There is hardly a single thing, name or concept to which they do not add '-tje' to make it sound cuter or more sympathetic. And it goes without saying that there is a café that claims to be the smallest in the city (if not on the whole European continent). Its popular name, of course, has the diminutive suffix: Het Doktertje.

The premises may be small – the space for guests amounts to a mere 18 square metres – but the establishment has a great tradition. De Dokter was founded by a surgeon from the nearby hospital on 2 September, 1798. Since that time it has been owned by the same family, the Beens. Generations of them have stood behind the counter here. Jannie and Jan, the ones currently doing their duty here, have been serving customers for 40 years.

As the name of the café suggests, for a long time De Dokter was the regular watering hole for doctors at a nearby hospital, which was merged with two other clinics several decades ago, however, and then moved to the edge of the city.

The beer served here is Grolsch (this is the Dutch brand characterised by its flip-top for opening and closing the bottle), and good house wines and various brands of whisky are also on offer. The acoustic background is music by old jazz and blues singers – Ella Fitzgerald or Billie Holiday, for example. It is also said that singers have performed live here. Presumably they played to a full house, which is less of a compliment than at other venues.

The café is located in a lively part of the city. Kalverstraat, a main shopping street, is very close, so if you decide to stop in at De Dokter, it may be a case of 'out of the frying pan and into the fire', at least in terms of the bustling environment.

And if this should get on your nerves, fortunately there is a quiet green oasis only 100 metres away: the Begijnhof.

Address Rozenboomsteeg 4, NL-1012 PR Amsterdam (Centrum) | Getting there Tram 1, 2 or 5 to Spui / Nieuwezijds Voorburgwal | Hours Wed – Sat 4pm – 1am | Tip La Mangerie (De Klencke 109) is run by apprentices. That may sound risky, but the idea works, and the food tastes good!

29___De Drie Fleschjes

Come in and try one

A 'proeflokaal' is a venerable, old-established institution in Amsterdam. The word signifies a café or pub where customers can try or sample something. A proeflokaal is not intended to be a place where you can drown your sorrows in alcohol, but an opportunity to widen your horizons and enjoy good company. A brewery or distillery is often part of the establishment, and some are even said to have their own vineyard (which must, however, be a fair distance away from its proeflokaal). In past times, liqueurs and genever were the specialities of a proeflokaal, but today they increasingly concentrate on brewing their own beer. Proeflokaal is not a registered concept: theoretically it would be possible to tear open a carton of wine from a discount supermarket, serve it in a hut, and call the whole thing a proeflokaal. Tradition and experience are therefore valued all the more in this business.

De Drie Fleschjes opened on 29 June, 1650. Rembrandt was still alive and active, memories of the Thirty Years' War were fresh, and there were surely plenty of good reasons for having a drink. The tavern belonged to a distillery, and the rows of oak barrels stacked along the walls still testify to this. Locals can rent casks to fill up with their favourite spirit.

De Drie Fleschjes makes no effort to be old or historic – it is old and historic. Among its oddities are the 'burgemeesterflesjes' (mayor bottles). Since 1591 every mayor of the city has been commemorated on a bottle. But the drinks menu has much more to offer, from aardbeienjenever (strawberry gin) to zoef-zoef – rum with crème de menthe.

The world outside may have changed many times over the centuries, but De Drie Fleschjes has remained as it always was: a haven of peace. Throughout its existence, it has always had regular customers who appreciated the qualities of the tavern. But new guests are also always welcome.

Address Gravenstraat 18, NL-1012 NM Amsterdam (Centrum) | Getting there Tram 1, 2, 5, 13, 17 to Nieuwezijds Kolk | Hours Mon–Sat 2–8.30pm, Sun 3–7pm | Tip Bar Bukowski at Oosterpark 10 is a hotspot in the often overlooked east of the city.

30__Engelbewaarder

A guardian angel for lonely hearts

Joseph Roth didn't really know where he belonged. His homeland, the old dual monarchy of Austria-Hungary, which he commemorated in literary form with his *Radetzky March*, no longer existed, and when people asked about his father, Roth used to say that he had hanged himself. He found this version less embarrassing than the truth: his father had lost his mind, which was not really astonishing in an age when the world had been turned upside down. Roth's fate took him from Vienna to Berlin, where he was successful but always remained an outsider. The reason that he was such a good observer is perhaps that he never felt part of his surroundings, wherever he was.

Joseph Roth loved Paris and would like to have stayed there as a correspondent, but that was not possible for long. When the Nazis took power, he had to flee. Once again he felt uprooted.

Among the few places that were like home to Joseph Roth were cafés such as Engelbewaarder. The Benelux countries were kind to this alien. Dutch publishers continued to produce editions of his texts. In Ostend he was able to meet Stefan Zweig, who didn't drink half as much as he did, but was twice as pessimistic. In bars and cafés like this, Roth was among like-minded people. Among people who, like Humphrey Bogart in Casablanca, would have answered the question 'What's your nationality?' with 'I'm a drunkard.' And if it was Joseph Roth's lucky day, the novelist Irmgard Keun would come along. She could not only write, but could hold almost as much drink as he did.

Today Engelbewaarder ('guardian angel') is still a good café. There may not be so much literary talent among the customers as there was in Roth's day (although you can never be sure about this), but there is still a literary programme. And jazz. And there are still things in the world that bring cares and sadness. And there is still something to drink.

Address Kloveniersburgwal 59, NL-1011 JZ Amsterdam (Centrum/Nieuwmarkt) | **Getting there** Metro 51, 53, 54 to Nieuwmarkt | **Hours** Mon–Thu 10–1am, Fri & Sat 10–3am, Sun 11–1am | **Tip** Schiller (the name says it all) on Rembrandtplein is a café for those with literary ambitions today.

31__The Entrepots

A coveted home in a warehouse

In the IJ, to the right of the Centraal Station, lie three man-made islands. Bickerseiland and Realeneiland are so-called because their owners made such a huge fortune on Caribbean islands that they were able to create islands of their own back home. The third is called Prinseneiland, not because it belonged to the Dutch royal family but because a house that once stood here was known all over the city as the 'Three Princes House'. The building that bore this name was demolished in 1800, but other structures that have given this district its reputation are still standing.

In the Golden Age of trade for the merchants of Amsterdam, the city had more than 800 warehouses, of which 100 stood in this area alone. Until World War II it was an industrial and commercial district. Products were bought at low prices and then stored until – God willing – they could be resold at a profit. When there was no work and no loading or unloading of goods, the area was abandoned and empty.

This changed after the war. The numerous industrial plants that operated here alongside the old warehouses were no longer welcome so close to the centre of a modern city. When the factories disappeared, the wares to fill the storehouses vanished too. The district gained a new purpose as a residential quarter, and the warehouses were converted, becoming sought-after homes. Their cellars were made into garages. The first residents were allowed to take part in designing their quarter, and in the first years, the rent of the flats was 300 to 400 guilders per month. For this price, you get nothing more than a door handle today. Prinseneiland, in particular, is regarded as a tip for insiders, as it has something like a rural atmosphere in the middle of the urban bustle. You feel you have been taken back to a time when no one imagined what changes would result from the discovery of the New World.

Address Prinseneiland, NL-1018 Amsterdam (Centrum) | Getting there Tram 3 to Harlemmerplein | Tip For fans of architecture: the 'Pyramids' are two imposing buildings at Jan van Gaelenstraat 1–29. From a distance they really do look like structures from Ancient Egypt.

32 __ Escape
Dance all night, perhaps with Prince

Escape is the 800-pound gorilla among the clubs of Amsterdam: the very biggest. There is no agreement on the numbers. Some speak of a capacity of 2,000 people. Others think this is an exaggeration and estimate that the club holds 1,500 (though, when asked, they don't exclude the possibility that it can be extended to take 2,000 guests). Yet Escape's beginnings in the 1980s was not especially propitious. The club was opened with a live television show, but it was broadcast on a cable channel, Skychannel Europe, viewed mainly in hotels by people who could not get to sleep, and in an era when channel-hopping was still a novelty. Besides that, the producer of the show was unable to find a suitable presenter, despite extensive casting, and had to make do with his sister in the role.

A few years later the sister, Linda de Mol, was one of the big stars in Dutch and international television, and Escape was one of the big attractions on Rembrandtplein, with cool young things flocking there to dance the night away. There are still some visitors to the club who love to tell of the occasion when Prince and his crew took to the dance floor here after giving a concert in the city.

At times the queues at the entrance were so long that they stretched all the way to the Tuschinski Theatre. Unkind people even scoffed that Escape had only been opened so that people who could not get inside Roxy and iT would still have a place for their night out. But that is unfair.

In the meantime, Escape has passed its 25th birthday and appears to be unstoppable. It has survived all the fashions and trends that arrived, and disappeared again, in the two-and-a-half decades since it first opened its doors.

Not many of the city's dance palaces can point to such a record – most of them had to close when the tide of fashion on which they rose had ebbed away again.

ZATERDAG	_____	23.00 - 05.00 UUR
ZONDAG	_____	23.00 - 04.00 UUR

Address Rembrandtplein 11, NL-1017 CT Amsterdam (Centrum) | **Getting there** Tram 4, 7, 9 or 14 to Rembrandtplein | **Hours** Thu & Sun 11pm–4am, Fri & Sat 11pm–5am | **Tip** Rembrandtplein, like Leidseplein, is a place where you can go from one place of entertainment to another just by falling over, so look around and let the mood take you.

ESCAPE
Club

Huisregels

1. U dient tenminste 21 jaar te zijn en dient dit, in geval van twijfel, middels legitimatie te kunnen aantonen.

2. Onze gasten dienen een verzorgd uiterlijk te hebben. Bijvoorbeeld: geen sportkleding of sportschoenen; geen kapotte kleding; geen onzedelijke kleding; geen petjes; geen vuile kleding of onverzorgd uiterlijk.

3. Van onze bezoekers verwachten we een tolerante en positieve houding ten opzichte van andere gasten die tijdens een clubnacht aanwezig zijn, ongeacht hun afkomst, cultuur, geslacht, seksuele gerichtheid, godsdienst en leeftijd.

4. Wij behouden ons het recht voor groepen groter dan 4 personen te weigeren.

5. Bij specifieke thema-avonden wordt de speciale dresscode middels flyers, pers en onze website bekend gemaakt.

6. Vanaf 1 juli 2008 geldt in Escape een algemeen rookverbod volgens de op die dag ingaande nieuwe wetgeving. Overtredingen op het rookverbod resulteren in een sanctie. Tevens worden eventuele proces-verbaal kosten verhaald op de overtreder.

7. Het is ten strengste verboden in Escape drugs, in de ruimste zin des woord, in bezit te hebben, te gebruiken en/of te verhandelen. Er zal hierop worden gecontroleerd. Bij constatering van overtreding van dit verbod zal per direct een LOKAALVERBOD gelden. Bij constatering van handel zal de politie hiervan in kennis worden gesteld.

8. Het is ten strengste verboden wapens, in de ruimste zin des woord, in Escape in bezit te hebben. Alle wapens worden in genomen.

9. Bij het binnentreden van Escape verklaart u zich akkoord met het ondergaan van een veiligheidscontrole. Toegang wordt pas verleend na deze controle.

10. Bij calamiteiten dient u TE ALLEN TIJDE de instructies van het personeel op te volgen.

11. De directie aanvaardt geen aansprakelijkheid voor enig letsel en/of vermissen/beschadiging van goederen.

12. Indien het binnen te druk is of op grond van een speciaal uitnodigingsbeleid drukte wordt verwacht, behouden we ons het recht u de toegang te weigeren.

13. Escape geeft volledig uitvoering aan het rookbeleid, ingaande 1 juli 2008. Het is alleen toegestaan te roken in Escape in de daarvoor bestemde rookkamers. Indien u rookt buiten de rookkamers kunt u gesanctioneerd worden.

14. Bij gedrag dat door andere bezoekers als hinderlijk, bedreigend, intimiderend of ongewenst wordt ervaren, volgt eerst een waarschuwing en daarna- bij herhaling- volgt verwijdering. In dat geval wordt ook in de toekomst de toegang ontzegd.

De ESCAPE directie.

33__The Ets Haim Library

In the beginning was the word

The Ets Haim Bibliotheek, which means the Library of the Tree of Life in Hebrew, is the world's oldest Jewish library. It was founded in 1616, when it was part of a larger educational project. Sephardic Jews who had been expelled from their homes on the Iberian peninsula after its reconquest by the Spanish monarchy had two aims: on the one hand, they wanted to preserve their rich cultural heritage, and on the other hand the library was meant to help them integrate into Dutch society. The holdings of the library include 30,000 printed works dating back to 1484 and 500 manuscripts dating back to 1282. Most of them can now be viewed on microfiche or in MMF format. The works provide a good survey of the world of ideas in the 17th century, but also include many specialist works from that period on such diverse subjects as history, linguistics, medicine and economics.

As a great trading city at that time, Amsterdam was a good location for establishing a library. Its new material prosperity resulted in a flourishing cultural life. A lively literary scene emerged, in which highly regarded poets wrote dramas and tracts, and were honoured even though they found little recognition abroad. Amsterdam was one of the few cities in Europe that guaranteed freedom of speech and the press – no small advantage as a place to live in during a period when not only unacceptable books, but also their authors, were burned.

Since 1675 the library has been housed in the buildings that surround the impressive Portuguese Synagogue, which was built at a time when Roman Catholic churches in Amsterdam still had to be disguised.

In 1889 David Montezino, then the librarian of the Ets Haim Bibliotheek, bequeathed his personal collection to the institution. For this reason it was sometimes known as the Livraria Montezinos. In 2003 the library was included in the UNESCO list of World Heritage sites.

Address Meester Visserplein 3, NL-1011 RD Amsterdam (Centrum) | Getting there
Metro 51, 53 or 54 to Waterlooplein | Hours By arrangement: +31 (20)4282596 | Tip At
Sint Antoniesluis 24 stands a monument called Grenspaal: a tortoise with a column rising
from its back. This sculpture dating from 1986 is intended to symbolise the long
and laborious work of reconstruction.

34__EYE

Lots of films from the Netherlands

Most people who travel to Amsterdam reach the city via Centraal Station. The trains from the airport arrive here, and 99.99 per cent of all passengers then leave the station on the south side.

In this direction they come to the canals, the city centre and almost all its attractions. The north side seems desolate and empty by comparison, a situation that is the reason for its nickname: Siberia.

However, on this side too there are some interesting things to look at. One of the newer attractions here is the film institute EYE, which was opened in 2012 by Queen Beatrix. EYE holds the biggest collection of films in the Netherlands: more than 46,000 of them, as well as half a million photos, tens of thousands of cinema stills, and screenplays. Exhibits from both Dutch and international cinema are collected.

This is a good opportunity to recall how great the Dutch contribution to movie history has been – one that dates back as far as 1895. In the 1970s, the image of Dutch cinema was marked by sex films such as *Emmanuelle*. In the 1980s there was a scandal around Maruschka Detmers and the first-ever fellatio scene in a mainstream film.

The best-known protagonist from cinematic circles in the Netherlands is probably Paul Verhoeven, whose career path matches that of other European directors who found their way to the USA. After his first success in 1973 with his bittersweet love story *Turkish Delight*, he went to Hollywood, where he made a star of Sharon Stone in *Basic Instinct*, but also, with *Showgirls*, produced one of the finest unintentionally funny films – thought by some to be the worst movie ever. His cameraman Jan de Bont followed him to America, was involved in the cult comedy *Ruthless People*, and took the director's chair for the movie *Speed*. More recently, Erik-Jan de Boer won a prize for the extremely lifelike animation of the tiger in *Life of Pi*.

Address IJpromenade 1, NL-1031 KT Amsterdam (Noord), www.eyefilm.nl | **Getting there** Ferry from Centraal Station to Buiksloterweg | **Hours** Mon – Fri 10am – 10pm, Sat & Sun 10am – 11pm | **Tip** Nieuwendammerdijk, a typical old Dutch street with pretty captains' houses, is also on the once-disdained north side.

35 __ The Faralda-Kraanhotel
Above the clouds

Thirteen is not necessarily an unlucky number. Crane number 13 was one of the many cranes that marked the skyline of Amsterdam's port on the north bank of the IJ. When the shipyards closed down one by one at the end of the last century, the cranes, too, gradually disappeared from view. The vision of the city's rulers was to make the district into a kind of creative adventure playground. Shipyard halls were to be turned into studios and workshops, and as artists usually like to put themselves on show, it was intended that visitors would be able to watch them at work and thus ensure footfall on the part of the public.

This worked very well, and still does – but no artist was crazy enough to install a studio in a crane. This is why they were scrapped – all of them except the above-mentioned number 13. And then Edwin Kornmann Rudi, who sees himself as a property developer for daring projects, came along. The crane was dismantled, taken to a special workshop in Friesland for alterations, and then brought back.

Before the crane could be used for accommodation, several technical problems had to be solved. Working cranes sway violently in the wind, for example. They are meant to do so, but hotel guests are less keen. Sanitary issues also had to be addressed. When a crane operator has to use a toilet, he descends to ground level or looks around for a bottle, but such an attitude to personal needs can hardly be expected of hotel guests. The last question to be answered related to legal problems: can a moving crane really be regarded as a piece of real estate?

In 2014 the hotel was opened, and alongside its airy, elevated position it has the advantage of not being a stressful or hectic place even when it is fully booked. There are only three rooms, each of them 35 square metres in size. The prices match the height of the structure: exorbitant.

Address NSDM-Plein 78, NL-1033 WB Amsterdam (Noord), www.faralda.com | **Getting there** Ferry 903, 905 or 906 from Centraal Station | **Tip** The A'dam Lookout at Overhoeksplein 5. In fact, it's no more than a swing with a glass floor that was placed on the roof of the former HQ of Shell to make it more than 100 metres tall. You can have fun here if you don't suffer from vertigo.

36_ The Ferries across 'het IJ'

Commuting over the waves

At first sight, Amsterdam presents two different faces to its visitors: the picturesque and cute appearance of the city with pointed gables of its canal-side houses has helped to make it world-famous, as has the garish, fleeting world of the Red Light District right next to the central station, where many promises are made, some of them cheap but none for free.

In neither of these areas do you usually gain any insights into the everyday life of the city. An Amsterdam for tourists is on offer. It fulfils expectations, while hoping to earn money as easily as possible in doing so.

To get a glimpse of the real Amsterdam, you can take one of the five ferries across the river. Even if there is nothing that you want to do on the other side, the trip across is worthwhile in itself. Each of the ferries has space for almost 250 passengers, who either leave the ship in haste with their bikes and mopeds, or crowd aboard with equal urgency. If you want to be cool (and in a certain age group, who doesn't?), you ride your scooter straight into the passenger cabin and leave the engine ticking over for the entire duration of the crossing, even though – or precisely because – this is actually prohibited.

The ferries run every few minutes, and to pass the time while you wait, there is usually a performance by one of those characters who wander around complaining loudly, here as on other open spaces in the city, and are not taken seriously by anybody. But none of these noisy hangers-around ever gets on board the ferry.

The passengers are what constitutes the normal public away from the entertainment quarters and tourist traps: managers, students, workers, office employees, home-office workers, apprentices and school kids.

The ferries, like the other local transport services in Amsterdam, run from about six o'clock in the morning until after midnight. And the trip is free of charge.

Address De Ruijterkade, NL-1011 Amsterdam (Centrum) | Getting there The main ferries depart by Centraal Station | Hours Timetable information: www.9292.nl | Tip If ferries are typical of Amsterdam, riding a bike is typical of Holland, of course. You can hire them at a reasonable price from Starbikes (De Ruyterkade 127).

37__Funny Photo Shoot
A window on the world of sin

Amsterdam's Red Light District is possibly the only place where men go window-shopping. Many things are allowed here, but taking photographs is not welcome and indeed not allowed. It is, admittedly, questionable how far this prohibition can be enforced in the age of smartphones, and there is also one place here where photography is not only permitted but desired: Funny Photo Shoot.

The idea is a simple one. There is a window that looks just like the other windows close by. Anyone who wants can take a seat there and be photographed. There are several different versions of this offer. If you book a 'vluggertje' (which could be translated as a 'quickie'), you can put on a wig and then sit in the window for the photo. In other variations you choose a sexy costume in the studio and have yourself styled, or even pose for a series of burlesque motifs.

There are many takers for this service, including couples, girlfriends and whole groups of women who want to add a touch of spice to their ingredients for a hen party and take away some unusual and unforgettable memories – because it goes without saying that group photos can be booked.

It is nothing more than a bit of fun, tongue in cheek. It should be emphasised that this business idea is merely playing a game with the ambience of the Red Light District, and is free from any kind of salaciousness. The owner, Walter Funken, and his partner are proper photographers who want to give their customers an amusing experience. And if anyone should fear that a photo of themselves sitting in the window might get into the wrong hands – not out of the question in the age of Facebook and Twitter – the road is blocked for a moment while the photo is taken, and any uninvited onlookers are shooed away. No one need worry that the situation will be misunderstood by visitors strolling around the district with specific intentions.

Address Sint Jansstraat 35, NL-1012 HG Amsterdam (Centrum), www.funnyphotoshoot.nl | Getting there Tram 4, 9, 16, 24, 25 or 26 to Dam | Hours By arrangement: +31 (20) 7724167 | Tip The Erotic Museum, Oudezijds Achterburgwal 54, provides further insights into the sinful and sensuous history of this district.

38_ The G. Perlee Organ Museum

Turn and turn again

Some people can't get enough of them, and others can hardly bear the sound: the hurdy-gurdy street organs of Amsterdam. Yet they are an established part of the street scene, and the repertoire of these instruments is surprisingly large. They play evergreens, Beatles songs and popular hits. Striking, colourful images cover the surface of the instrument, and marionettes dance at the front of the organ, bringing the songs to life as the music plays.

Every piece has a special accompaniment: the rhythmic rattle that the 'organist' makes with the tin in which he collects contributions after his performance. In a way, it is possible to regard these organs as early, bulky forerunners of the iPod and its relatives, as they played music whenever the owner wanted to hear it. Every sound that the instrument generates is a note created by a hole punched into a strip.

In the first half of the 20th century there were well-known composers who wrote their music only for this instrument. Gijs Perlee and Leon Warnies, the founders of the museum, themselves come from families that have a long tradition in making hurdy-gurdies.

Originally the street organ comes from Italy, but it was brought to perfection in Amsterdam. At its peak, up to 30 instruments were on the streets at any one time to entertain the citizens and their guests. In those days, the custom was that as soon as the last note had died away, residents would throw a few coins out into the street, wrapped in paper so that no one would be injured by them.

In the museum, treasures from the past are cared for and, if necessary, restored. Anyone who would like to hire an organ along with its organist can do so here – an unusual feature for all kinds of parties. And if you have a neighbour whom you would like to annoy for a while, then hiring a hurdy-gurdy for a session at home might just fit the bill.

Address Westerstraat 119, NL-1015 LZ Amsterdam (Jordaan) | Getting there Tram 3 to Marnixplein | Hours By appointment only: +31 (20)6249310 | Tip For more musical instruments from bygone days, you can visit the Pianola Museum, a few houses further on at Westerstraat 106.

39 _ Glowgolf
How to see in the dark

There must be many people who have complained that crazy golf quickly gets boring. But their laments had no effect. For when the time is ripe for a great idea, then some enterprising person emerges to bring about the great transformation that humanity has been longing for – and that is exactly how glowgolf was born.

Glowgolf is crazy golf in a closed space. It is played in the dark. Now this could be boring after a while, so the room is illuminated with black light. While players move through the room in small groups (a maximum of five players per group can be accommodated), underwater creatures appear out of the darkness. The player who succeeds in hitting their balls into the jaws of sharks and other submarine holes has reached the next level.

Next up are the dinosaurs. If you have succeeded at all the holes here, the grand finale then takes place in the jungle. A total of 15 psychedelically coloured holes are played. It is fascinating to see how, thanks to the lighting in a simple room that has been blacked out, a completely different world is created. You have never seen a crazy-golf course like this one.

The visual impression is strongest if the whole team dresses in white. And if this does not seem challenging enough, you can make it all even more surreal by trying to play the course while wearing 3-D glasses.

There are good reasons to believe that glowgolf could become a new trend in sports. It all began a few years ago in a small multi-purpose hall in a rural area, where customers could try skiing in winter and drive a go-kart all year round.

Originally, glowgolf was simply intended to be an alternative use of the hall while alterations were being carried out. However, the idea really caught on, and at present hardly a month passes in the Netherlands without the opening of a new venue for this crazy sport.

Address Prins Hendrikkade 194, NL-1011 TD Amsterdam (Nieuwmarkt) | Getting there Bus 22 to Kadijksplein | Hours Sun–Wed 11am–9pm, Thu 11am–11pm, Fri & Sat 11–1am | Tip On the subject of new trends: at De Ruyterkade 153, LED bowling adds a new twist to an old sport by means of special lighting in the ceiling.

40__The Heineken Experience

A kidnapping with consequences

The Heineken Experience is an event staged by the world-famous beer producer in a former brewery. If I am informed rightly, visitors are given a guided tour past copper-coloured brewing vats, and at the end are treated to two glasses of beer and possibly a baseball cap in corporate colours. This experience is extremely popular, and many people book it. I have not taken part in it myself, because I see no reason why I should play the part of the waiter and have to walk to and fro myself when I order beer. Besides that, after many years of experimenting on myself I have come to the conclusion that the effect of ale does not depend on how much you know about the methods used to make it.

A different kind of Heineken Experience, one that was more like a horror story, took place shortly before seven o'clock in the evening on 9 November, 1983 in the offices of the company management. Gangsters kidnapped the managing director, Freddy Heineken, and his driver.

The ordeal of the kidnapped people lasted three weeks. They were hidden away in a hut in the harbour district. The crime attracted a great deal of publicity at the time. A ransom equivalent to 16 million euros was handed over. Subsequently, the police succeeded in tracking down the criminals and arresting them in France, but then the usual legal tug-of-war began, with attempts to have them extradited and the engagement of celebrity lawyers. Of course, this topic was of great interest to the media. Various books about the case were published. Films were made, too, and some still hope that Hollywood will take up the subject.

Of the two kidnappers, at least one gained a dubious kind of celebrity, and gets mentioned from time to time in the media even today for a variety of reasons. But this does nothing to mitigate the crime he committed – and for that reason his name will not appear here.

Address Tweede Weteringsplantsoen 21, NL-1017 ZD Amsterdam (Centrum) | Getting there Tram 12, 16 or 25 to Weteringscircuit | Tip If you need a drink after this horror story, you will find the customer-friendly Heineken Experience opposite, on Stadhouderskade.

41__Henri Willig Cheese Cellar

A cellar full of dairy products

Everything here looks exactly the way you always imagined. Henri Willig's cheese cellar is a low vaulted space in the basement of the building that was once the headquarters of the United East India Company, the Dutch trading company founded in the 17th century that had commercial activities across the globe. Here, two adjacent shops sell genuine treasures for lovers of cheese.

There is cheese of various ages for customers of all age groups. Some are made from cow's milk, others from sheep's or goat's milk, as well as smoked cheese of various kinds, flavoured with many different spices. And customers are encouraged to try samples before buying. What all these kinds of cheese have in common is that they come from the Gouda region and from a farm that is open to visitors. The two large whole cheeses by the entrance are only there for decoration, but anyone who enters and discovers a new variety can stock up. Tourists like the small cheeses weighing 350 grams. But if you want and you are able to carry it, you can purchase one or more whole cheeses with a weight of four-and-a-half kilos.

Although the interior of the shop presents a very traditional impression, Henri Willig's cheese shop is not an old-established company. Its beginnings can be traced back to 1974, when wooden clogs were produced alongside the cheese-making activity. Now the company is entirely devoted to cheese, but the principles established over 40 years ago still apply.

The company headquarters is in Frisia, in the town of Heerenveen, but production is organised on a regional basis. The cheese-making methods are meant to be as green as possible, and customers can not only see the cheese being made, but can also influence the type of products that are offered. Henri Willig is constantly innovating to keep coming up with new kinds of cheese that take account of consumers' preferences.

Address Singel 516-518, NL-1017 AX Amsterdam (Centrum) | Getting there Tram 1, 2 or 5 to Koningsplein | Hours Daily 9am–8pm; Dec–Mar Mon–Thu 10am–5pm, Fri–Sun 10am–6pm | Tip De Bakkerswinkel at Zeedijk 37, in the genuine style of an old Dutch bakery, is also worth a visit.

42__ The Hilton Hotel
Legendary highs and lows

The history of this building clearly tells what became of dreams of love and peace. On 25 March, 1969, John Lennon and Yoko Ono began their so-called 'bed-in for peace' in suite 702 shortly after getting married. The Beatle Lennon had separated from his first wife Cynthia and from the first great love of his life (the Beatles). He was in urgent need of a new challenge.

The bed-in lasted a week. Many representatives of the press came and stayed a long time, but their hopes of witnessing live sex were disappointed – John and Yoko kept their pyjamas on the whole time. And there were no other sensations. The newly-weds were really only interested in promoting peace. The Vietnam War continued for a few years, however, and there was no end to violence in other parts of the world.

On 27 June, 1991 the Amsterdam Hilton made headlines again. This time, the reasons for the publicity were much less peaceful. On the lawn in front of the hotel, the drug king Klaas Bruinsma was shot by a hired killer from the Yugoslav mafia. On 11 July, 2001, shortly before 2.30 in the morning, the artist Herman Brood jumped to his death from the roof of the hotel. A suicide note was found in the inside pocket of his jacket, containing a single sentence meaning 'Now have a good party'.

Brood was known internationally as a musician and had married the German singer Nina Hagen in the years before his death but he had gained a reputation in the Netherlands as a painter – despite the handicap of being colour blind. After his death, macabre as this sounds, the value of his paintings increased considerably.

Recently the Hilton Hotel was included on the Dutch list of heritage monuments. This is official recognition of its status as an outstanding building dating from the middle of the 20th century. The hotel management was presumably pleased to make the headlines with some good news at last.

Address Apollolaan 138, NL-1077 BG Amsterdam (Zuid) | **Getting there** Tram 5 to Apollolaan | **Hours** Reservations: +31 (20)7106000 | **Tip** A must for architecture fans: the Apollohal is an impressively graceful and airy basketball hall in the style of the Amsterdam School.

43__ The House with the Waterfall

If water below is not enough

There is no shortage of water in the Netherlands. There is the North Sea, there are rivers and canals, lakes and ponds, not to mention the fact – it has to be admitted – that it also rains fairly often. But for some Dutch people, all of this is not enough. The architect Hans Hagenbeek seems to be one of those people.

The building that he designed stands in a quiet side street near Nieuwmarkt, and is truly attractive. Its architectural form reminds some people of a building on the Piazza del Campo in Siena. And if this occurs to you too, then you are on the right track, as this was the architect's intention. Of course, the version in Amsterdam is not quite as large and doesn't have the same breathtaking view, but it is an original notion, competently executed.

Perhaps this similarity to a square in Tuscany would have sufficed to make the building well known, but in fact a second feature has brought it to wider public attention. The large glass façade at the front of the building serves as the backdrop for an artificial waterfall that flows down the panes of glass into a marble-clad pool. The marble gets covered with graffiti scrawls now and again, but fortunately that does not diminish the effect. The falling and splashing of the water is an entertaining spectacle – especially on sunny days, when the silhouette of the tower of the Zuiderkerk, which stands opposite, is reflected in the glass of the façade. However, if you would like to enjoy the sight and sound of the stream of water splashing down the wall of the building, you will need a little luck. When the weather is frosty, the waterfall does not operate, for understandable reasons. Who needs a simulation of a burst water pipe on days when there are enough genuine ones? And when the weather is very hot, too, the waterfall might be switched off and the splashing interrupted for a while.

Address Zuiderkerkhof, NL-1011 WB Amsterdam (Centrum) | **Getting there** Metro 51 or 54 to Nieuwmarkt | **Hours** Viewable from the outside only | **Tip** The sundial on the Nieuwe Kerk on Dam had a special significance for a long time: until the end of the 19th century, all the clocks in the city were set from it.

44 — Hofje van Wijs

Tea, coffee or Me?

Although today the Netherlands is a state whose surface area seems so small on most globes that the name of the country usually has to be abbreviated, it was once a global power. The original name of New York was Nieuw Amsterdam, and it might easily have stayed that way. The Australian island Tasmania, by contrast, is still named after its Dutch discoverer, as is the Barents Sea. The pearl of the Dutch overseas possessions was present-day Indonesia, which was long known as the 'Dutch East Indies' until the Indonesians gained independence and decided to use their own name.

On the long journey to Asia, the Dutch stopped in Ethiopia, where they made the acquaintance of a previously unknown plant. The place where they discovered it was called Kaffa. The plant was taken to the botanical garden in Amsterdam, where it was cultivated and propagated. The organisation behind this and other activities was the Dutch East India Company, which was something like the first globally operating enterprise. The issue of shares meant that the risk of its ventures was spread and borne by many, and that Dutch merchants from the hinterland provinces, Gelderland and Groningen, could also participate in its success.

When King Louis XIV of France visited Amsterdam he was presented with a coffee plant, which later indirectly found its way to Brazil.

In the Golden Age, the Netherlands was the leading importer of tea and coffee. Different kinds of tea were traded at a special tea exchange in Nes, where many theatres are situated today. Whereas 'proeflokaale', where drinkers can try out alcoholic spirits, have existed for a long time, for tea and coffee there is Hofje van Wijs. This café and shop is dedicated to a tradition with an equal love of detail. All those who discover a new favourite blend there can order a delivery, or take it home with them straight away.

Address Zeedijk 43, NL-1012 AR Amsterdam (Centrum) | Getting there Tram 4, 9, 16, 24, 25 or 26 to Centraal Station | Hours Mon & Tue 4–10pm, Wed–Sun noon–11pm | Tip The Mokum museum café at Kalverstraat 92 is also worth a visit. The theme here is not so much colonial as city history.

45_De Hollandsche Manege

In the saddle at the heart of the city

In this location you would not expect to find something so high-class. De Hollandsche Manege is the country's oldest riding school. Its first forerunner existed as long ago as 1744, and the present neo-classical style building was constructed in 1882 on the model of – what else? – the Spanish Court Riding School in Vienna. It is no coincidence that the manège, i.e. the enclosure in which horses and riders are trained, is sited right next to Vondel Park, as the park was once often used as a place in which to go horse riding.

The building is characterised by its steel roof girders, glass dome and gallery for spectators that encircles the manège. In view of this architectural splendour it may sound unbelievable, but in the 1970s an equestrian gentleman called Joop Rittmeester (riding master) van de Kamp wanted to pull the building down and construct a new manège in the Amsterdamse Bos. Outraged horse lovers fortunately blocked this plan. The Hollandsche Manege was spared, and underwent a thorough restoration in 1986.

There is stabling for 35 horses and 15 ponies. For those who can ride, everything is possible here: hiring a horse, taking riding lessons, learning how to groom and saddle a mount, joining a riding excursion, and so on.

If you can't ride a horse, you can take part in a workshop instead to learn about equestrian sport, and possibly to discover the horsey person that has long been dormant inside you. And then you could do all the things that riders do.

If, on the other hand, your conclusion after the workshop is that horses, seen close up, are simply very large, have a huge rump and also smell fairly pungent, then you can still hire the manège for a party. And if that overstrains your budget, then the alternative is to drink a cup of coffee and watch the riders on their horses. Murmuring that you could join in. If you really wanted to.

Address Vondelstraat 140, NL-1054 GT Amsterdam (West) | **Getting there** Tram or 12 to Eerste Constantijn Huygensstraat | **Hours** Daily 10am–5pm | **Tip** Het Woeste Westen (The Wild West) at Overbrakerpad 3 is an adventure playground for children – with raft trips instead of horses.

46__The 'In Coignac' Façade Stone

In vino veritas – carved in stone

A few hundred years ago the stones set into walls and façades were the equivalent of house numbers for people who could not read. They looked amusing, were colourful, and provided information about the profession of the house owner. Some of them were adorned with a proverb, often a strange one. In the old quarter of Amsterdam, many of these stones have survived. You could base a whole tour of the city on them. There is the 'robber' (Elandsgracht 73), 'the ship with two men and a dog' (Karthuizerhof at Karthuizersstraat 21 – 131) and 'the writing hand' (Egelantiersstraat 52) to name just a few.

For a book it would be fitting, of course, to say more about the 'writing hand', but unfortunately we do not know much more. It is said to have belonged to a schoolteacher called Hendrick Wient who lived in the 17th century – and that is all. Whether he was a good teacher, or took no care in his job and was only interested in the hand of the beautiful daughter of the mason who carved the façade stone – the old pedagogue took all the answers to the grave.

But there is one stone about which we do know more. On the house with the address Geldersekade number 97, between the first and the second floor, is a small relief with the inscription 'In Coignac'. The house was built in the 17th century and belonged to a wine merchant named Willem Hendrickszoon. This is exactly the period when a man from Amsterdam is said to have invented Cognac. First the Dutch imported salt from Cognac, then excellent wine that they liked to drink but often did not travel well – until an apothecary from Amsterdam hit on the idea of warming the wine, then adding water and spices to it. The result, now called brandy (from the Dutch 'brandewijn', meaning a wine that has been 'burned', i.e. distilled), could be kept longer and is a success to this day.

IN COIONAC

Address Geldersekade 97, NL-1011 EM Amsterdam (Centrum) | **Getting there** Metro 51, 53 or 54 to Nieuwmarkt | **Tip** If you want to look more deeply into the subject of alcoholic spirits, try the Tales & Spirits cocktail bar at Lijnbaanssteeg 5 – 7.

47___Ikea

If you are careful, nothing will be crooked

(You can assemble this article yourself by combining the paragraphs that follow. Please take note of the diagram attached. If any components are missing – commas, dashes, dots – please contact the manufacturer directly, not the publisher.)

Of course, there is no special reason why you should go to Ikea when you happen to be in Amsterdam. The stores look identical all over the world. They treat their customers the same way there as they do at home. And *köttbullar* Swedish meatballs are *köttbullar* Swedish meatballs wherever you go.

Nor can Ikea Amsterdam claim to have any superlative that is unique to this store. It is not the biggest branch of the furniture chain (the largest are in Sweden and China), and it is not even the first to be opened outside Scandinavia (that was in Zurich, in 1973, one year before the company started in Germany and Japan). Ikea came to Holland relatively late. In 1982 a store opened in Amsterdam on Stadhouderskade. It only sold small items, and you had to order the rest from the catalogue. It was only in 1985 that Ikea moved to the present location in the south-east of the city, which has been expanded and altered several times.

Despite its Swedish origins, Ikea is a proper Dutch firm. Two, to be exact. Inter IKEA Systems B. V. in Delft owns the concept, while INGKA Holding B. V. in Leiden runs all branches worldwide. Delft is where company managers are trained. The reason to move from the Nordic forests to the west European lowlands lies simply in Dutch tax law, which allows global companies to conceal and complicate their structures so that the balance sheet, revenues and profits are only apparent to insiders. Other companies also take advantage of this: Amsterdam has the largest number of company headquarters in Europe.

A popular Dutch publication is entitled, translated: Why no one pays taxes (apart from you). Just to let you know.

Address Hullenbergweg 2, NL-1101 BL Amsterdam (Zuidoost) | Getting there Metro 50 or 54 to Bullewijk | Hours Mon–Sat 10am–9pm, Sun 10am–6pm | Tip If you are looking for something special to furnish your home, you will find the opposite of the Ikea style at Tike Design, Grimburgwal 15.

48__Jimmy Woo

An oriental mystery man

The art of self-presentation, looking stylish for the fashionable scene, is cultivated and appreciated in Holland generally and in Amsterdam in particular. Most people try to style themselves as harmless citizens aspiring to be part of a nice, staid idyll.

Nevertheless, egos and vanity are as marked here as anywhere else, as you can tell from the fact that the Dutch continually have to reassure their fellow citizens that their success, of whatever kind, has not changed them in any way at all. Though success is relative. There are a few Dutch people whose international reputation was only a brief episode, but who report to the national media about their huge triumphs abroad (and of course about how they have remained normal people despite these achievements).

Alongside all of these demonstrative displays of sobriety and modesty, however, there is also a great longing for glamour. And a few years ago Caspar Reinders, an impresario from the entertainment business, showed how to satisfy these desires. He is not from Amsterdam, but from nearby Amersfoort, and has always had a weakness for Chinese antiques. Following the demise of the cult clubs RoXY and iT, he hit upon an idea about how to fill the gap they had left. Extensive googling led him to the conclusion that, among the global 1.3-billion population of Chinese, not a single one answers to the name Jimmy Woo. He therefore invented this fictitious person and spread a rumour that the said Jimmy Woo wanted to found a club in Amsterdam.

The strategy was an unmitigated success. The media clamoured for interviews with the mysterious club founder, and since it opened in 2003, Jimmy Woo has been among the city's trendiest addresses, with its oriental décor and great club programme. They have the strictest door bitch you ever saw, although quite what the club's policy is remains a bit of a mystery.

Address Korte Leidsedwarsstraat 18, NL-1017 RC Amsterdam (Centrum) | Getting there Tram 1, 2, 5 to Leidseplein | Hours Thu–Sun 11pm–4am | Tip Suzy Wong, opposite and smaller, has a similar name and concept.

49___Johan Cruyff's Birthplace
The cradle of world football

Betondorp (Marbletown in English – no, sorry: Concreteville) is a district in the east of Amsterdam. Its official name is Tuindorp Watergraafsmeer. It was constructed in the 1920s, and, as the nickname that it quickly acquired suggests, is an early example of concrete-built housing.

The official reason given for this style of architecture was that the authorities wanted to find out whether it was possible to manage without the ubiquitous red bricks that were otherwise used in the city. The fact that bricks were extremely expensive in those years undoubtedly played a part in this decision.

All of this would scarcely deserve mention – if a certain Hendrik Johannes Cruijff had not been born here on 25 April, 1947. He was better known to contemporaries and admirers as King Johan. He was a long-haired beanpole who played without shin pads and never pulled up his socks. In those days his father had a greengrocer's shop.

Compared with other football greats such as Pelé and Maradona, Charlton and Beckenbauer, Cruijff did not win many international trophies. He was, after all, Dutch, which means he had a hereditary tendency to finish as runner up. Nevertheless, he is regarded as the inventor of modern football: 'Voetbal totaal', 'total football', as this style of play was named when it was showcased at the World Cup in Germany in 1974. Essentially this involved attacking the other side before they even left the dressing room and playing them into a state of dizziness. Cruijff took this philosophy to Barcelona, who paid a world-record fee for him, and where his playing style was further refined and became a widely admired ideal.

Until his death in 2016, Johan Cruyff was the nation's strict moral authority for football. After news of his death was released, the match between the Rotterdam clubs Feyenoord and Sparta was interrupted in the 14th minute in memory of his shirt number.

Address Akkerstraat 32, NL-1097 XN Amsterdam (Oost/Watergraafsmeer) | Getting there Tram 9 to Brinkstraat | Tip The Ajax Experience on Rembrandtplein is overhyped and commercial, like so much in modern football, but useful as a crash course in the club's history.

50_Johnny Jordaanplein
Amsterdam's Greenwich Village or Shoreditch

Jordaan is an old quarter of Amsterdam – some say it is the most famous quarter. The name Jordaan is said to come from the French word 'Jardin' (i.e. garden), but no one knows for sure. The most famous resident of the district – surprise, surprise – was Rembrandt. The quarter lies between the canals Prinsengracht, Lijnbaansgracht, Brouwersgracht and Leidsegracht. In the 19th century it was the most densely populated and the poorest part of the city. There were repeated revolts, with fatalities.

But even in Jordaan, gentrification has taken hold. It is a deeply fashionable quarter. Almost 13,000 homes are currently occupied by approximately 20,000 people, so there is nothing like overcrowding today. However, Jordaan's old reputation lives on. The cramped living conditions and the numerous conflicts led to a culture in the district that was expressed in songs.

One of the best-known singers from this area was called Johnny Jordaan. He started his career in the 1950s as a singing waiter in Café De Kuil and was discovered in the 1960s.

Typical songs by Johnny Jordaan have a big accordion part and vocals that are reminiscent of Italian *bel canto*. The tempo is usually medium fast, with a jazz brush swishing softly across the skin of the drum, and in your mind's eye you see streets, deserted early in the morning, where a lonely road sweeper is brushing the cobblestones with a broom of twigs.

Johnny Jordaan earned a lot of money and lost it again, was in debt to the tax authorities, went abroad, came home again, and died in 1989 at the age of 65 following a brain haemorrhage. Outside the Netherlands his music did not attract much attention, but in his homeland he remains an idol to this day. Which is why, in the district that he came from, the local council has dedicated a square to his memory that looks like a cross between a monument and a shrine.

51 The KamerMaker

Architects' dreams in 3-D

When MP3 files were invented, the music industry declined the researchers' suggestion that they should include protection against copying in the code. We all know what happened next: the end of the CD, wailing instead of singing, and outsized live concerts that look more and more like mass gymnastics. Then films ended up on the internet, then books, and so on.

Experts are now predicting that soon everyone will be able to download templates for anything that they want to print. And anyone who still thinks this is a figment of the experts' imagination should take a look at the latest project by an Amsterdam architectural practice.

DUS Architects was founded in 2004, and the company specialises in 'public architecture': designs that are ambitious artistically and structurally, and that provoke. 'Kamer' means a 'room', and the KamerMaker is a pavilion for three-dimensional printing with which the company is aiming for the sky. As we 3-D printing experts know (to keep the conversation going, we'll just pretend to be experts), the most widely used 3-D printer is the so-called Ultimaker. We still say so-called just as we possibly used to say, a long time ago, that we had a so-called mouse to operate the computer. In contrast to an Ultimaker, the KamerMaker is as big as a house and can print houses itself.

From an organic material, layers one millimetre thick are printed and then piled one on top of the other. The first project was a column two metres tall, and then DUS Architects became ambitious. The idea was to produce an entire typical Dutch canal house from the printer. The result can be visited at the address on the opposite page, and anyone who thinks this is all a game might like to remember how everything began with MP3 files and so on. Perhaps the day when we will download our houses from the internet is not far distant.

Address Tolhuisweg 2, NL-1031 CL Amsterdam (Noord) | Getting there Ferry from Centraal Station to Buiksloterweg | Hours Tue–Fri 1–5pm, information at www.dusarchitects.com | Tip For more on this subject, visit the museum Het Grachtenhuis, Herengracht 386.

52 _ Karpershoek
The oldest corner pub in the city

Diagonally opposite Centraal Station lies Karpershoek, an immovable rock in the torrent of tourists that swirls around it, yet strangely ignored by most of them. This makes no difference at all to Karpershoek. It has seen a lot of people come and go.

Karpershoek is the oldest pub in the city. Its date of foundation was long thought to be 1629, but then documents turned up to prove that taxes were being collected from the tavern as long ago as 1606.

Thanks to the revenue authorities it was then possible to assert with even more justification than before that Karpershoek is 'de oudste kroeg van Amsterdam' (the oldest tavern in Amsterdam).

'Oe', by the way, is spoken in Dutch like "oo' in 'food', and the word for a tavern is therefore pronounced like 'kroog', and Karpershoek rhymes with 'spook'. Originally the pub had a different name, but nobody knows what this was. Since 1922 it has been in business under the name Café Karpershoek. Two generations of the family owners made the restaurant successful, until in 1972 they reached the end of the road. Renovation of the building was necessary, and that would have been too big a strain on their financial resources.

The premises were therefore sold to a property development company, which would probably have converted the site to a completely different use. But this did not happen, as the farewell and memorial celebration for the pub's closing turned into a protest meeting. And when the municipal tram company finally threatened to close the tram stop outside Karpershoek, the storm of outrage was so great that the new owners backed off. They restored the pub and carried on running it under the previous name, Karpershoek. But the old walls and wooden beams don't care a bit about any of these events. Having been around in the world as long as they have, they know that 'a rose by any other name would smell as sweet'.

Address Martelaarsgracht 2, NL-1012 TP Amsterdam (Centrum) | Getting there
Tram 1, 2, 5, 13 or 17 to Martelaarsgracht | Hours Mon–Thu, Fri & Sat 7.30–2am,
Sun 7.30–1am | Tip Café de Sluyswacht (Jodenbreestraat 1) is also very old and crooked,
but most important: the bar stands up straight.

53__KattenKabinet

No more than a cat deserves

Bob Meijer opened KattenKabinet in 1990, a few years after his beloved cat John Pierpont Morgan passed away. The pussy, whom good friends were allowed to call 'J. P. Morgan' for short, lived from 1966 to 1983. You could say that the pet had a long and fulfilled life. Every year on his birthday, the cat was given an unusual present. Mostly this was a portrait. But there is also a bronze bust, and if the story is true that J. P. sat still to model for the bust, then that would be most remarkable.

Unfortunately, John Pierpont Morgan died before his owner could move into the new house. To ensure that the memory of the noble animal did not fade, a whole storey of the building was devoted to commemoration. The theme of the exhibits is cats in general, but it goes without saying that J. P. Morgan has a prominent place. Alongside normal portraits there is a dollar bill, though bearing the head of a cat instead of a deceased American president. The place that normally bears the message 'In God We Trust' on a dollar bill has the following inscription in J. P.'s version: 'We Trust No Dog'.

The cat museum consists of five rooms on the *piano nobile* of the house. There is a big parlour and a music room. All of it is stylishly equipped with elaborate upholstered furniture and wallpaper. What an enterprising cat could have done to all of this on a good day – well, that hardly bears thinking about. Let's just say that the rooms and their furnishings are a delight, not only for cat lovers but for everyone who takes pleasure in beautiful things.

The aim of the KattenKabinet is to illustrate the influence that cats have on the life of humans, and the interaction between people and animals. But it is not revealing too much to state that the symbiosis between one particular person and his feline friend is illuminated in a particularly impressive way.

Address Herengracht 497, NL-1017 BT Amsterdam (Centrum) | **Getting there**
Tram 1, 2 or 5 to Keizersgracht | **Hours** Mon–Fri 10am–5pm, Sat & Sun noon–5pm |
Tip Poezenboot at Singel 38, a home for stray cats, is grateful to anyone who will give
a new home to a cat.

54_KNSM Island

Building strange bridges

The Dutch are fond of abbreviations, and some of them – like KLM – are good ones and easy to remember. Others are less successful. KNSM, for example. It stands for Koninklijke Nederlandse Stoomboot-Maatschappij (Royal Dutch Steamship Company), but is also the name of an island that, not unusually in Holland, is man-made. It takes its name quite simply from the fact that the Koninklijke Nederlandse Stoomboot-Maatschappij once had its company headquarters here.

That is a long time ago. In 1977 the steamship captains left their island, but very soon after that squatters, artists and drifters took their place. Then the city government came along and turned the island into a residential area. In contrast to other islands in the harbour district, the working spaces of the former nautical occupants were integrated into the new housing, which makes it interesting just to stroll around the island, keeping your eyes open. Just as a suggestion.

The architect Sjoerd Soeters wanted to have something like a belt of canals like that in the city centre. So he had canals dug, crossed by bridges that are very different in style from those in the city. They were designed by the Belgian husband-and-wife artist team Monika Droste and Guy Rombouts. At first sight it seems you are looking at them through the bottom of a bottle, but in fact the bridges are surprisingly robust, and present no problems to pedestrians and cyclists.

And that is not the only cast-iron art that you can find here. On Barcelonaplein is an intricate hedge made from iron. Its name is Vensterhek. It too was created by a Belgian artist. Whether the southern neighbours of the Dutch wanted some kind of revenge on their brothers to the north, or simply needed to let off steam while they were working away from home – it's hard to say. But both of these works are undoubtedly impressive.

Address Across the bridge of Zeeburg, NL-1019 Amsterdam (Oost) | Getting there
Tram 10 to Azartplein | Tip *Volten's Knot* at Grasweg 10 (on the other bank) is also an
interesting work of art, and the name tells you what to expect: a huge steel knot made
by an artist called Volten.

55___Kraak Café De Molli

Controversial occupying forces

Much of the Netherlands lies below sea level. Part of the identity and pride of the country – in contrast to that of a certain larger neighbour, whose name we need not mention explicitly – is that you expand by claiming land from the sea instead of invading other countries. This attitude deserves respect, of course, but it also has consequences. If the dams and dikes should ever be breached, then the land will be under water. Regardless of this fact, the Dutch are not more concerned about climate change than other nations. Their interest in home ownership remains unaltered, and no one seems to be afraid of flooding and the resulting loss of property. However, in this context it is not difficult to appreciate that people who simply occupy buildings instead of paying for them cause bad blood.

The squatter ('kraak') movement reached its first peak around the time of the coronation of Queen Beatrix (see ch. 38), when the slogan 'Geen woning – geen kroning' (no home – no coronation) was heard for the first time. The battles over occupied houses, often violent, continued into the 1980s, died down for a while, and then came back to life with the dawn of the new millennium.

Dutch politicians tried various ways of getting a grip on the problem. There was a hard line and a soft approach, there were house-building programmes to relieve the housing crisis for young people, and finally – surprising for a country like Holland – a so-called kraak ban was passed.

Kraakcafé De Molli is a cosy neighbourhood meeting place and the oldest of its kind in Amsterdam. It opened in 1979 and, apart from serving food and drink, puts on a varied art programme, as well as providing a surgery to advise potential squatters – because they still exist. When Queen Máxima and her Willem moved into their villa in Eikenhorst, the neighbours – squatters – were already there.

Address Van Ostadestraat 55 HS, NL-1072 SN Amsterdam (Oude Pijp) | **Getting there**
Tram 3 or 12 to Ruysdaelkade | **Hours** Tue–Sun 9pm–1am | **Tip** Three streets further on
is a shop that represents a completely different philosophy: Blond (Gerard Doustraat 69)
sells products connected with – well, blonds.

56 The Kraanspoor Building
Laid across the tracks

Although it looks like a high-rise that has fallen over, the Kraanspoor (crane track) Building is a functioning office block. The site was originally occupied by a crane that moved on rails in order to load freight wagons. NDSM (see ch. 67) commissioned the construction of this huge installation in 1952, but the demise of the docks meant that the crane lost its purpose. This happened in the late 1970s. Twenty years later, shortly before the start of the new millennium, an architectural practice was awarded the task of designing a new office building for the site.

The decision was taken to use the steel structure of the former moving crane as a foundation and to put the building on top of it, in the place where the crane had once moved to and fro.

The dimensions of the new building are impressive. 270 metres long, glazed all round, 13 metres wide and some 15 metres high. Inside it are 12,000 cubic metres of office space, all of it occupied entirely by nice colleagues, because people who sit in a glass house don't throw stones.

Imposing as the building is, the technical challenges that had to be overcome to construct it were great. The all-round glazing could have made the interior as warm as an oven when the sun shines. To prevent this, an ingenious system of double-glazed panes was devised that generates currents of air at the edges of the building and helps to cool it. Whereas the inner panes cover the walls of the structure, the outer ones are variable and can be adjusted. In addition, through a pump, water can be taken from the river for cooling.

Construction of the Kraanspoor Building commenced in 2006, and it had been completed just a year later. That is an impressive achievement, like much else about this building, which stands out for its ingenuity and apparent simplicity. It has justly been awarded many architecture prizes.

Address Ms. Oslofjordweg 40, NL-1033 SM Amsterdam (Noord) | Getting there Bus 391, 394 to Stenendokweg | Hours Viewable from the outside only | Tip The Muziekgebouw aan het IJ on the other side of the river is also impressive for its architecture and has a lovely terrace.

57 Lieverdje

Publicity and provocation by the Provos

Originally this small statue of an Amsterdam boy, a street vendor, was little more than a publicity measure by a cigarette manufacturer. And then the slightly built lad became part of a cultural war that had a big influence on the campaigning of the 1960s.

The monument called Lieverdje was unveiled on 2 May, 1959. It was made by a sculptor called Carel Kneulman and paid for by a cigarette maker called Hunter, and at first everyone was perfectly content with it. The artist was pleased to gain such a commission. His patron had the advantage of getting subtle publicity for his business, and the citizens recognised some of their own qualities in the cheeky little boy, who was a loud-mouth but had his heart in the right place.

Then Robert Jasper Grootveld made his entrance. Grootveld described himself as an anti-smoking magician, and started a one-man campaign against the cigarette industry. He scrawled the letter K on tobacco advertising (in an English-speaking country it would have been a C: for cancer) and threw currants at the Lieverdje sculpture. His activities got an enthusiastic reception from the Provos (the Dutch name for the rebellious students of 1968), who adopted and refined them.

A few decades later, the European Union would probably have given him a medal for this kind of activity, but back then, the police reaction showed no sense of humour. They felt they were being provoked and clamped down hard. The Provos in turn thought this was a provocation by the authorities, and so the situation escalated. It culminated in the proclamation of the Free Orange State on the square.

The Free State is long since forgotten, and the campaigner Grootveld died a few years ago. In 2012, Lieverdje was toppled – but there was no political or other motive. A delivery truck collided with him. One month later, the boy had been repaired and replaced on the same spot.

Address Spui, NL-1012 WX Amsterdam (Centrum) | Getting there Tram 1, 2, 4, 5, 9, 16, 24 or 25 to Spui | Tip On the paving of Marnixstraat, between the bars Lux and Kamer 401, is a stone ladybird. It was installed here and in other places where people fell victim to violence.

58__Mail & Female

For women only

It may come as a surprise to some to learn that mail-order firms specialising in erotic products did not exist in Holland as early as in some other countries. It was not until 1988 that the first mail-order business providing erotic items for women was founded: Mail & Female. The women who started it got the idea while visiting a sex shop in the Red Light District. They were interested in the subject and were far from being repelled by all that was exhibited in the shop. What did not appeal to them, however, was the atmosphere, and something else they found lacking was competent service. They wanted better information than the boasts about potency that usually adorned the packaging. The founders of Mail & Female would have liked a shop where they felt at ease and where, instead of crude comments, they were offered some good advice and first-hand reports based on experience of the products.

No such shop existed in the Netherlands, even in cosmopolitan Amsterdam, so they decided to set up a company themselves. Their mail-order business was soon successful. They were overwhelmed by customers' reactions. Obviously they had discovered a gap in the market: erotic equipment for women, presented in a way that appeals to women.

The change in presentation also had consequences for the product range. Soon the company had its own products in the catalogue, and exerted influence on the materials and the design of the bought-in items. This is not surprising. A sex toy that is only intended to fulfil a male fantasy for 10 minutes (or in some cases even less) has to meet different demands from one that makes a woman feel at ease and also gives her pleasure. As time passed, the product range of Mail & Female became more daring. Because for the women behind the brand, the focus is on two things above all: to satisfy needs, and to stay curious.

Address Nieuwe Vijzelstraat 2, NL-1017 HT Amsterdam (Centrum) | Getting there Tram 7, 10, 16, 24 or 25 to Weteringscircuit | Hours Mon–Sat 11am–7pm, Sun 1–6pm | Tip On a similar theme: Drake's Lingerie Boutique, Damrak 61.

59 _ Maria Sibylla Merian
Kiss of the Spiderwoman

Maria Sibylla Merian was a remarkable woman. She was not afraid of spiders. When her female contemporaries would often run away screaming, Maria Sibylla reached for a sheet of paper and a pencil. In making her drawings she was extremely precise and extremely thorough. She also had plenty of time on her hands because, although her husband liked women, he did not want much to do with his own wife.

Maria Sibylla Merian was born in Frankfurt in Germany (where her image used to adorn the 500 deutschmark note), but in 1691, via an indirect route, she arrived in Amsterdam. At that time Amsterdam had 200,000 inhabitants. It was the third-largest city in the world and the centre of a commercial empire that encompassed the globe. As a result of various tragic events (her brother and mother had both recently died), Merian had to make a contribution to the family income. So she drew flora and fauna with her characteristic accuracy. Her books were a great success. Even Tsar Peter the Great, who was staying in the city, bought some of them. Maria Sibylla found the transformation of a caterpillar to a butterfly especially fascinating. To find out which butterflies emerged from which larvae, she even bred caterpillars. Perhaps she did not realise that she herself was undergoing a metamorphosis.

Vijzelstraat is usually stated to be her place of residence in Amsterdam. According to Ella Reitsma, who wrote a book about Maria Sibylla Merian and her daughters, her final address was Kerkstraat. Thanks to Harmen Snel, a hard-working employee of the city archive, it was possible to ascertain the number of the house where she lived. We note this detail only because in other publications about Amsterdam – including those from notable publishers of travel guides that shall remain nameless here – there is no reference whatever to her place of residence.

Address Kerkstraat 115, NL-1017 GE Amsterdam (Centrum) | Getting there Tram 1, 2, 5 to Prinsengracht | Hours Viewable from the outside only | Tip If you would like to immerse yourself in Merian's world visit the Hortus Botanicus (Botanical Garden), Plantage Middenlaan 2A.

60 Marriage for a Day
A trial run in white

Las Vegas is a city devoted to entertainment, with services of the horizontal variety – but is also popular with couples planning to marry. Many famous people have travelled there to tie the knot – and in many cases got their divorce again only a few days later.

As far as the first of these topics is concerned, Amsterdam too has a certain reputation. And the city is also catching up on the second matter.

For a few years now, it has been possible to book a lightning wedding here. And in comparison with Las Vegas, there is one indisputable advantage: here, all those involved know from the very outset that it is not meant to be taken seriously. Not much of the (impressive) ceremony makes a permanent mark, except for a photo that you attach to the fridge. As the organisers put it: 'Even if the marriage does not last, the feelings can remain.' (In real life it is often the other way round.)

A wedding for a day costs 75 euros and takes place in a proper church, for example the Posthornkerk. There is a bridal dress in the old-fashioned style, a veil, lots of plastic flowers, rings, music and a red carpet. The wedding dresses are available in all the usual sizes, while for the men, suits and top hats are at the ready. Of course, there is also rice for onlookers to throw and someone to take your picture. If desired, the ceremony can be held in English.

The idea arose in connection with Koninginnedag, 'Queen's Day', originally as a joke, but when the idea was revived around Valentine's Day, it quickly became popular. It would be wrong to assume that this is a way of laughing at the momentous institution of marriage. It is not so uncommon for this ritual, greeted with a giggle by all participants, to become truly serious in the end. The demand continues to be high, at any rate. The company has been in business for 10 years, and that is longer than many marriages last.

Address Eerste van der Helststraat 15, NL-1073 AB Amsterdam (Zuid/De Pijp) | Getting there Tram 16 or 24 to Albert Cuypstraat | Hours For information see www.wed-and-walk.com. Bookings can be made for any day between 10am and 10pm. | Tip De Emaillekeizer at 1e Sweelinckstraat 15 is an old-fashioned shop for household goods where you can buy everything for setting up a home, from saucepans to a rolling pin.

61_ The Max Euwe Centre

The world champion from Holland

The 20th century was an age of great chess duels. As most people recall it, these confrontations always worked out as follows: a lot of earnest people gathered around a chess board, and in the end a Russian won. There was only one exception to this rule, when in 1972 Bobby Fischer surprisingly triumphed, but then success went to his head and he lost his sanity.

This point of view is not quite right. There was another 20th-century chess player who succeeded in breaking through the ranks of the all-conquering Russians. Machgielis – Max for short – Euwe was a genuine Amsterdamer, who competed in his first chess tournament at the age of 10. His hour of greatness came in 1935. In a hard struggle, he defeated the flamboyant Russian Alexander Alekhine, who had previously been regarded as an unbeatable genius. Two years later Euwe was forced to surrender his title, but he continued to play chess. Among other activities, he wrote a book about how to learn the game of chess, which differs from others in this genre in that it is actually readable. Until his death in 1981 he remained active as an official in the World Chess Federation.

Among the successors to Euwe, the Netherlands could not boast a further world champion, but did produce several outstanding players. Jan Timman was probably the best of them. The legacy of the world champion is maintained in the Max Euwe Centrum. In front of the entrance is a monument depicting the master as a modest man, just as he truly was for the rest of his life. (To this day Euwe is the only amateur who ever succeeded in winning the world championship.) Next to it in the paving is an outsized chess board on which other talented amateurs play out toughly contested games, with the Amsterdam Hard Rock Café in the background; surrounded by spectators who of course know exactly what the players are doing wrong.

Address Max Euweplein 30a, NL-1017 MB Amsterdam (Centrum) | Getting there Tram 1,
2 or 5 to Leidseplein | Hours Tue–Fri & first Sat in the month noon–4pm | Tip If you like a
game but are not keen on chess, try your luck in the neighbouring Holland Casino.

62_Mellow Yellow
The original coffee shop

(A monologue by someone who is in the know.) 'Just cool it, friend.
Anyway, I don't aim to get excited about anything much today. And
besides, the thing isn't worth arguing about. I mean the question
of who was first. It may be true that Bulldog advertises itself as the
oldest coffee shop in town. Although that isn't the right choice of
words: coffee shops aren't allowed to advertise at all. All the same,
on a branch of the Bulldog chain you can read "the oldest coffee
shop in town" or something like that. Don't expect me to go and
check up on it. It is equally a fact that Mellow Yellow opened back
in 1973. It was in a different street then, but the name existed, and
that's when the whole thing started. Along came a guy who you
knew had something with him. He just happened to come by, you
understand? He was there every day and sat at the counter ... that
was a coincidence, you know? At first this was not particularly legal.
In 1976 things became easier. But even today, coffee shops are only
tolerated under strict conditions. For example, it is possible to take
over an existing shop, but you are not allowed to open up a new
one just like that.

And the result of all this is that today there are only about
200 coffee shops, whereas there used to be 500 of them at one time.
The same thing applies here as in other matters: if you think that
anything goes in Amsterdam, you had better check what you've just
been smoking.

But we need to establish one thing: Mellow Yellow was the first
coffee shop. At Bulldog they did not get started until 1975 at the
earliest, and if you don't want to believe it, then consider this: when
you get a licence for a coffee shop from the city authorities, they give
you a sticker, and Mellow Yellow's quite clearly has the number 001.
For ever, get it? Even though it had to close down on 1 January 2017.
Once and for all, seemingly. No shit, man...'.

Address Vijzelstraat 103, NL-1017 Amsterdam (Centrum) | Getting there Tram 12, 16 or 25 to Weteringscircuit | Tip If you want to see a legendary place from inside: Rusland (Rusland 16) also claims to be the oldest coffee shop in town, and it is still open.

63__ The Museum Tram

A trip for transport nostalgics

A normal journey on a tram in Amsterdam is not especially enjoyable. You do reach your destination, but in general the tram spends more time at a standstill than in motion. The museum tram is a completely different matter. In summer it runs every Sunday from Haarlemmermeer Station to Amstelveen Bovenkerk.

When the first museum tram went into operation in summer 1975, it travelled only a few stops. Today's route, over a distance of seven kilometres – to the edge of the Amsterdam Forest – is approximately as long as a 'normal' tram line run by the city transport authority GVB (Gemeente Vervoer Bedrijf). The museum tram is operated by two societies that – just as modern traffic policy prefers – take care separately of the rolling stock and the tracks.

The EMA (Electrische Museumtramlijn Amsterdam) is the one responsible for the tracks. It ensures that the tram cars, despite their advanced age, are not derailed and arrive safely. This non-profit organisation does not possess a single tram – these belong to a different society, called RETM (Rijdend Electrisch Tram Museum).

In the course of years, the tram enthusiasts have collected and restored historic tram cars from various European countries. This means that you might encounter a genuine Viennese tram (see photo) while wandering through Amsterdam. However, the main focus is on Dutch rolling stock – and above all on models that once passed through the streets of Amsterdam.

When passengers, presumably simply intending to enjoy the ride, get aboard the tram, they are greeted by organisers who take their activity very seriously. They even have a mission statement, in which they explain why they take the controls in the driver's cabin. For them it is about preserving the mobile heritage of the country and keeping it moving on the roads, and making it possible for people today to experience this part of their history.

Address Amstelveenseweg 264, NL-1075 XV Amsterdam (Zuid) | Getting there Tram 16 to Harlemmermeerstation | Hours See www.museumtramlijn.org for information, including a printable timetable | Tip It is worth taking a trip on the Metro: below ground, at rush hour, Amsterdam really does look like a proper city.

64__Museum Vrolik

A true chamber of horrors

Rembrandt is not only the famous painter of *The Nightwatch*. He also painted *The Anatomy Lesson of Dr Nicolaes Tulp*. In the picture you can see the doctor standing over the dissected body of a poor man who obviously failed to state clearly enough in his will that he did not wish to donate any organs. Opposite the doctor is a group of physicians who are obviously not squeamish, as they are following the lecture and the incisions of Dr Tulp with evident interest. Some of them actually paid to be included in the painting.

In the Roman Empire they would probably only have cut up a corpse to determine who should be the next emperor, but in the Renaissance, when humans were once again at the centre of attention, there was a desire to know more exactly what the inside of a body looked like.

Gerardus Vrolik was a successor to Dr Tulp, a professor of anatomy. Whenever he found an abnormal skull, he put it on a shelf at home. His son Willem shared the father's passion. He pursued the same career, and also continued his father's hobby of collecting. (It would be great to know what the two of them looked like. Perhaps they regarded the items in their collection as attractive and perfectly normal.) Both of them took a delight in deviant embryos and anatomical abnormalities that are difficult for an onlooker to stomach. The exhibits are, however, by no means merely a cabinet of curiosities. Thanks to cutting-edge molecular analysis, their old specimens can still be of use to science today.

The collection of father and son Vrolik later passed into the ownership of Amsterdam University, where it can be visited in surroundings that are appropriate to a display of body parts. All those who are interested in anatomy can spend a few enjoyable hours here. Anyone else who goes there should think carefully beforehand what they should eat for breakfast.

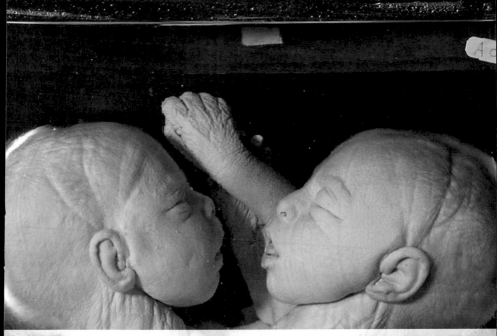

Address AMC (Academisch Medisch Centrum), Meibergdreef 15, NL-1105 AZ Amsterdam (Zuidoost/Harlemmermeer) | Getting there Metro 50 or 54 to Holendrecht | Hours Mon–Fri 10am–5pm. Note: not suitable for children (seriously!), tours by arrangement: +31 (20)5664927 | Tip At Amstel 216 is a house covered in red scribbles. They are said to be the work of a 17th-century owner who drew them with his own blood!

65_ The Museumswoning

Live like the old Dutch

Tuindorp Oostzaan was once best known for the fact that the dike broke here. On 14 January, 1960, water flooded the town and drove 15,000 residents from their homes. It took almost 20 years to repair all the damage. The battle against water is part of the lives and historical ordeal of the Dutch people.

The tuindorp ('garden village') was a company estate. The people who lived here worked at the NSDM shipyard. When the shipbuilding operation closed down, and the areas surrounding it were also scheduled for demolition, a completely intact house interior dating from the 1920s with its furnishings was revealed by chance.

When this turned up, the feelings of its discoverers were as if they were excavating the ancient city of Pompeii. An era that was familiar from tales told in the family, from films and from newspapers, but whose everyday life was by no means as thoroughly documented as our own happenings in the age of Facebook and the internet, could now be visited and examined in every last detail – from the baby's high-chair with a chamber pot to the coal-fired stove and the family photos on the wall.

The Museumswoning ('museum home') was built in 1922 by a construction company and is now administered and cared for by a non-profit foundation, which ensures that everything is maintained 'the way it used to be'. Exhibitions and films about this lost era are also shown in the old home.

Dutch visitors come here to see how their grandparents and great-grandparents lived. They can look at a furnished bedroom with its wardrobe and a child's cot, the kitchen with pots and pans and cupboards, and a bathroom in which household cleaning items, flat-irons and a glass case filled with old packaged consumer products are on display – an opportunity to get to know the Netherlands in a way where you would least expect surprises: in daily life.

Address Meteorenweg 174, NL-1033 HJ Amsterdam (Noord) | **Getting there** Bus 35, 37 or 363 to Plejadenplein | **Hours** Seasonal opening, see www.historischarchief-toz.nl/ Museumwoning.htm | **Tip** Further reminders of the days when the shipyard was a world of its own are the warehouses on Silodam.

66__NAP
The water line

When people in countries bordering on the Netherlands talk about the weather, rainfall and flooding, they are talking about Amsterdam without knowing it. The reason is the Normaal Amsterdamse Peil, NAP for short, also known as the Amsterdam Ordnance Datum, which was also adopted in other western European countries as the base measurement of sea level for measuring water levels and altitudes.

For Holland, the 17th century was not only the Golden Age, but also a period of many floods. After a particularly severe storm tide in 1675, the people of Amsterdam decided they had to act. They began to measure the water level and how it changed. The average water level measured from September 1683 to September 1684 has since then been taken as the zero reference point. If Amsterdam wanted to be safe from flooding, the dikes and dams had to be at least nine feet and five inches above NAP 0. To ensure that no one forgot this, Mayor Hudde gave instructions for it to be inscribed on eight large marble slabs that were attached to sluices and locks all around the IJ. This wise precaution proved its worth more than once, and the marble slabs were later called 'Huddenstenen' (Hudde stones) in honour of the mayor.

It took some time, but later other countries began to use this measurement system: Germany in 1879 and from 1973, when the SI unit measures were introduced, others followed. Thus the Netherlands, like France with the original metre measure in Paris, created a standard that is used across the continent.

Only one of the mayor's original Huddenstene still exists. It is on the Eenhoornsluis, a lock on the short Prinsengracht. You can take a photograph of it, but it is no longer used for measurements. For this purpose there are 50,000 measuring points across the Netherlands. One of them is beneath Dam, another on the Stopera building on Waterlooplein.

Address Amstel 1, NL-1011 PN Amsterdam (Centrum) | **Getting there** Metro 51, 53 or 54 to Waterlooplein | **Hours** The Stadhuis with its visitor centre is open Mon–Fri 9am–6pm. Between 10am–5pm the exhibition can be visited. | **Tip** If you come from an upland area, don't laugh: in the Amsterdamse Bos (see ch. 3) there is some higher ground, called Heuvel, with an altitude of no less than 10 metres above NAP. Mountainbikers love it.

67 __ NDSM Island
The other rainbow warrior

Another helping of alphabet soup. One more of those abbreviations. Here we go: NDSM stands for Nederlandse Dok- en Scheepsbouw Maatschappij (Netherlands Dock and Shipbuilding Company). NDSM was once the biggest shipyard in the world. Its site extended for more than two kilometres on the north side of the IJ, and when a big passenger steamer was launched from its slipway, the queen came to smash a bottle of champagne on the bows. The yard also built cargo ships, tankers and warships.

But like everything else in life, one day the end comes for a shipyard, too. Great efforts were made to breathe new life into this gigantic industrial landscape. Its final demise was postponed by means of mergers, loans and political assistance, but in May 1984 the game was over once and for all, and the company had no alternative but to go into liquidation.

Today there are still several repair works on the site, in addition to various cultural activities. The national boat fair is held here, and the quay is the mooring place for the Sirius, which used to be the flagship of Greenpeace (it was formerly owned by the Royal Dutch navy). The environmental activists acquired this former pilot boat in 1981 so that they could protest against the dumping of radioactive waste in the North Sea and transport of nuclear material to Scandinavia. They used it on voyages to Norway and Iceland to interfere with the culling of seals and whale hunting. Its last major mission was in 1998, against a ship that was carrying tropical hardwoods from endangered rainforests.

The boat is 46 metres long and more than 8 metres wide. Its top speed was 12 knots (approximately 22 kilometres per hour). Since 2001 it has been anchored at the quayside, without a screw. Tours are held for children. In the meantime, the ship that did so much to preserve the environment is in need of restoration itself.

Address Tt. Neveritaweg 61, NL-1033 WB Amsterdam (Noord) | Getting there Ferry from Tasmanstraat to the NDSM shipyard | Tip In summer a wide range of cultural events are held at the former shipyard. For information, see www.ndsm.nl/news.

68__Nemo

Knowledge is power (for children)

Nemo is one of the spectacular new buildings that have appeared in the harbour area in recent years. It is a round structure and looks a bit like a UFO that has unexpectedly landed on the earth. And this association is by no means far-fetched. The developers of Nemo succeeding in recruiting the architect Renzo Piano to design the building, fitting it in between his commissions to work at Potsdamer Platz in Berlin and on the Shard in London. It now accommodates the largest science centre in the Netherlands – five storeys, crammed with nerdy adventures.

The attraction is aimed at children and teenagers between the ages of 6 and 16 who want to explore scientific phenomena in a playful and interactive way. But adults are not prohibited from visiting and using the various installations.

There is lots to discover at Nemo. It includes an inventors' factory, a journey through the mind, a ball factory (where no balls are manufactured, however, but they serve to make industrial processes comprehensible). The biggest robot ever made walks through the building with hesitant steps, and gifted children can surely program it to give their older brothers a piece of its mind when they get pushy and want all the attention.

Although Nemo is about science and knowledge, the whole thing is conceived as a feast for the senses. You can inspect, touch and sniff at everything – and in some cases you can even taste the exhibits, for example if you want to try your hand at making liquorice.

By the way, the name of the science centre has nothing to do with Jules Verne or with fish from an animated film. It was opened in 1997, and its name back then was New Metropolis. However, with this title, the exhibition found little favour with the general public. It was only when the name was shortened to Nemo that people queued to get inside. Make of that what you will.

Address Oosterdok 2, NL-1011 VX Amsterdam (Centrum) | Getting there Bus 22, 48 or 359 to Kadijksplein | Hours Tue–Sun 10am–5.30pm | Tip Also for children, not as trendy as Nemo but hands-on: Ontdekhoek (Discovery Corner), Burgemeester Röellstraat 145.

69__The Noorderpark Pool

A world-class place to splash about

Cities that lie on a river and at some stage spread out on both banks are familiar with this problem: one side, usually the one that was settled more recently, gets a worse deal than the other. Examples of this are north and south London, in Berlin the district of Spandau beyond the river Havel, and no doubt in the Hungarian capital there are differences between Buda and Pest, even if a stranger does not know which is which.

In Amsterdam, for a long time, in fact for a period of centuries, the underprivileged side was the north. It was ridiculed as 'the place near Amsterdam' or 'the town nearby'. Tourists hardly ever found their way here, and many locals were proud to declare that they had never set foot in the north of the city.

In the 21st century this seems to be changing. The north is seen as hip, and is now attracting attention as an area of exorbitant rents. In truth, it was never half as awful in the past as people described it. The housing estates built for shipbuilding workers had a pretty, rural air. There was no comparison with the tenement dwellings built elsewhere. They were called garden villages (*tuindorps*), and between them lay parks like the Noorderpark, which was formed by merging the Florapark with the Volewijkspark.

There has been a swimming pool here for a long time, but after reopening in 2015, the eyes of the world were upon it. The Noorderpark pool was voted the world's loveliest public swimming pool. Prizes of this kind tend to be marketing ideas – nevertheless, the Noorderpark pool is beautiful. It is light and airy, with lots of wood and a catchment reservoir for rainwater, which is then used to fill the pool. Moreover, the surrounding park is also attractive.

It is doubtful if anyone will go to Amsterdam for the sake of this swimming pool, but if you are there anyway, it is definitely worth taking a look.

Address Sneeuwbalweg 5, NL-1032 VS Amsterdam (Noord) | Getting there Bus 34, 35 or 763 to Sneeuwbalstraat | Hours Check website as there are different times for leisure swimmers and sports swimmers: www.amsterdam.nl/sport/waar-sporten/zwembaden/ noorderparkbad/openingstijden | Tip In the north of the city you can take a trip into the surrounding area – to Ransdorp, for example, where amazing tales are told about a church without a tower.

70__The OBA
Book-heaven on earth

This must be what paradise would look like for librarians, beyond their wildest dreams, the ultimate product of unrestrained flights of fantasy. Here they got everything right. The library, which opened on 7 July, 2007 (the date was consciously chosen so that even non-readers could take note of it) is large and spaciously fitted out. A usable surface area of almost 30,000 square metres is available, proudly presented – surprisingly in a country that is accustomed to flaunting smallness – as the largest library in Europe.

The building is huge, the stocks (1.7 million books) impressive. The institution is also popular (3.5 million users), which may be due to the fact that the opening times are unbeatably visitor-friendly.

In the library interior, the prevalent atmosphere is enlightened and relaxed, and this feeling almost inevitably rubs off on the visitors. In the foyer is a piano, next to it a sign proclaiming, roughly translated: if you have mastered this instrument, then you are welcome to display your artistry, but if not, you are simply requested to refrain from making any noise.

Those who do not speak the Dutch language might object and say: what use is it to me to find a library that gladdens the heart of a reader in every possible way, if it disappoints me in one decisive matter: it has no books that I can read? But here, too, consolation is at hand.

First, the library has large stocks of foreign-language literature, second it has enormous holdings of recorded material and DVDs, and last of all, if the above is not persuasive enough, it has a trump card: on the roof of the building is a café and a terrace from where you have a breathtaking view of Amsterdam. So even if you don't want to read, there is enough to look at. And if this does not convince you to pay a visit, there are poetry readings, held in sign language for the deaf.

Address Oosterdokskade 143, NL-1011 DL Amsterdam (Centrum) | Getting there Centraal Station | Hours Daily 10am–10pm | Tip If you want to become an expert on viewing platforms in no time at all, try the one at the Doubletree Mint Hotels next door, and see what you think.

71__ The Okura Hotel

A huge barometer with a star

In the age of the great navigators and explorers, there was one country that stubbornly resisted the merchants and armed forces of the west: Japan. It was a very long time before, faced with the threatening presence of American gunboats, this empire opened its markets.

Before this happened, the long-nosed white devils faced many obstacles if they wanted to trade with Japan. Most of those who tried, failed. With one exception: the Dutch. They were permitted because they were regarded as an honoured exception amongst the arrogant would-be colonists. Even enmity during World War II failed to destroy the special ties between the Dutch and the Japanese.

I do not know if this was the reason why the city authorities of Amsterdam allowed the Japanese to build a hotel in the De Pijp district that exceeded the usual roof height many times over. By the standards of Amsterdam, the Okura is a kind of skyscraper. In Japan it is widely believed that certain rituals and rules help to avert bad fortune. Whether this holds true is a matter of debate (just think of the Fukushima disaster), but one thing is certain: the Okura Hotel has 23 storeys, and for the above-mentioned reasons of superstition, there is no 13th floor.

The building was opened by Prince Claus in 1971 and at that time, with a height of 75 metres, was the tallest in Amsterdam, though in the meantime it has been surpassed by the Rembrandt Towers Hotel on the Amstel.

Originally the Okura hotels were staff accommodation for the flight crew of the Japanese airline JAL. They have now been enhanced to the status of luxury hotels, and with their Japanese design exude an air of tranquil simplicity. The Okura in Amsterdam has one further special feature: the lighting on the eaves of the roof acts as a barometer that can be seen from afar: blue means good weather, green is bad, white is changeable.

Address Ferdinand Bolstraat 333, NL-1072 LH Amsterdam (Zuid/De Pijp) | **Getting there** Tram 12 or 25 to Cornelis Troostplein | **Hours** Reservations: +31 (20)6787111 or www.okura.nl | **Tip** The bar on the top floor is a popular location with a wonderful view of the city, truly a highlight.

72__The Olympic Stadium

Yesterday's laurels may not wither

The 1928 Olympic Games were the first at which an Olympic flame was lit. Whereas this task was given to a prominent person at later games, the ceremony in Amsterdam was carried out in the sober Dutch manner, even though it was a première: so the flame is burning, now get on with the sport! The torch parades that are now part of the show around the Olympic flame were not added until 1936, in Berlin, and both of these rituals are now an established part of the Olympics.

When Amsterdam was chosen as the venue in 1927, the architect Jan Wils was commissioned to build the Olympic stadium. Perhaps he would have preferred to do this for his home town, Den Haag, as the stadium he designed for Amsterdam was not an especially large affair. The building material, as at the Betondorp (see ch. 49) was concrete, which was given a cladding of two million bricks. Inside, the circular arena was right up to date, but from the outside, as several critics complained, it looked more like a fortress. And it does not accommodate very many spectators: fewer than 23,000. Since the 1928 games, the names of Dutch Olympic medal-winners have been commemorated, although not consistently. The tradition was started, then interrupted, and then it continued.

After the games, the stadium continued to be used for sporting events, including football, of course. It was the home ground of FC Amsterdam, while Ajax played in the De Meer stadium before moving to the ArenA in 1996. They only played in the Olympic stadium when there was a match in the European Cup or against their old rivals Feyenoord.

As Amsterdam is a city where there is always demand for more housing, in 1987 the stadium was scheduled for demolition. However, on second thoughts it was spared and restored at great cost. In 2018 an ice speed-skating world championship will be held there, and in 2028 perhaps even an Olympic Games again.

Address Olympisch Stadion 21, NL-1076 DE Amsterdam (Stadionbuurt) | **Getting there** Tram 16 or 24 to Stadionplein | **Hours** Viewable from the outside only, except during events | **Tip** The modern counterpart for sports is the Amsterdam ArenA.

73__ The Onbekende Canal

Monument for a waterway

If we start from the assumption that the early inhabitants of the Netherlands did not have all that much spare time, and we know that nevertheless they were continually digging, then there must be a reason why so many of their cities have canals, and also why they gave these canals the name 'gracht'. Why didn't they simply call them canals? Well...

'Gracht' comes from 'graft', which is related to the English word 'grave', and it means to dig – as in 'hard graft'. A gracht therefore designates a man-made waterway, on both sides of which buildings stand. There were many reasons to dig such a canal. First, a waterway was the cheapest and most effective means of transport. For a long time horses were luxury items, reserved to the nobility and to knights, and neither of these two classes was dominant in Holland, which had a rustic and bourgeois character.

Apart from this, a gracht was the forerunner of a sewer. And its final task, by no means an unimportant one, was defence. When towns were under attack, trenches and moats around forts and other defensive works could be flooded from the canals. This can be seen even today in the names: a slotgracht was a canal specially built for defensive purposes.

This military strategy was still being pursued in the first half of the 20th century, when it was believed that a gracht, if only it was wide enough, could bring a tank assault to a stop. But that was rarely the case.

In other cities there are monuments to the unknown soldier. In Amsterdam, where the gracht played a major role in the history of the city, it should not be thought astonishing that there is also a so-called unknown (onbekende) gracht. It can be found immediately behind the Carré musical theatre, and even has its own postcode. And considering that it is 'unknown', it has now become remarkably famous.

Address Lepelstraat, NL-1018 XP Amsterdam (Centrum) | Getting there Metro 51, 53, 54 to Weesperplein | Tip The 'gardens on the water' at Ruysdaelkade 70 are a floating mini-biotope for waterfowl.

74___The Oranje-Nassau Barracks

For men only

The Oranje-Nassau Barracks, with the longest façade in the city at 278 metres, used to be fairly untypical of Amsterdam. Women were not allowed in, and that had been the case for 200 years. Men, on the other hand, had to enter at least once in their lives, whether they wanted to or not, as all young Amsterdam males came here to be mustered for military service. They got a day off work while they were subjected to the usual procedures ('bend down and cough'), which was fantastic, but this single free day preceded a denial of liberty lasting a year and a half, which a lot of them thought was not so fantastic.

Construction of the barracks began in 1810, for Napoleon's army of occupation (as the Dutch called it) or for the French army of liberation (as Napoleon's people believed). The building, which was of impressive size by the standards of the time, had to be paid for by the citizens of Amsterdam, which they did with gritted teeth. Although it was expensive, carrying its cost was still better than having French soldiers quartered in their homes – soldiers who not only saw themselves as the rulers of the world but at that time (the Battle of Waterloo was still a few years off) really were ruling the world.

When the barracks was completed three years later, the French had long departed, so the Dutch army moved in. Until 1984 the barracks served its time in the male military world. When the army relinquished the building, the city authorities wanted to take it over. The government of the Netherlands agreed, but demanded a lot of money for the site. The arguments continued for a while until an ingenious archivist discovered that in 1867 the army had given a commitment to returning the site to the city of Amsterdam without charge after its use ended. This finally happened in 1989. Today a number of different companies have their offices in the barracks.

Address Sarphatistraat 600–660, NL-1018 AV Amsterdam (Centrum) | Getting there
Tram 10 to Alexanderplein | Hours Viewable from the outside only | Tip The nearby
Sarphatipark is a good alternative to Vondel Park.

75_The Oranjesluizen
Controlling the change of water level

The Oranje Locks form the border between the inner and outer IJ, where they regulate the water level in the North Sea Canal. The complex consists of three smaller locks for commercial shipping and for leisure craft, and one large one for big ships. Two exclusive through-passages are reserved for the use of fish.

The lock chambers have varying sizes. The biggest of them, which has been in operation since 1995, measures 24 by 200 metres. It is opened and closed from control rooms in two buildings that command a good view across the site, thus giving the lock keepers the ability to shout at the captains of leisure cruisers through a megaphone if they fail to manoeuvre in and out of the locks quickly enough.

The construction of the locks was initiated in the 19th century. Gradually the installations were extended. The separation of leisure boats from commercial traffic proved to be particularly beneficial to their smooth functioning. At present the locks are used by more than 60,000 recreational and 45,000 commercial vessels each year. For pedestrians and cyclists they are also useful as a bridge across the IJ, although they may have to wait a while if a large vessel is passing through.

Watching the operation of the locks can be a fascinating spectacle. After all, humans can play at being God here (by creating the world the way they want it to be) as well as the Man in the Moon (by managing the tides).

Locks can also be a source of involuntary comedy, for example when an amateur boat-owner wrongly judges the length of his ropes, only to find, when the lock chamber is drained and the boat is expected to fall according to the water level, that his vessel is left hanging in the air. But the most impressive aspect of the Oranjesluizen is their sheer size. In a country that does not have many monumental structures, they are like cathedrals.

Address Zuider IJdijk & Schellingwoude, NL-1023 Amsterdam (Noord) | **Getting there** Bus 30 to Ijdijk | **Hours** Only of interest for navigation | **Tip** The Lloyd Hotel (Oostelijke Handelskade 34) was the final accommodation in Europe for many emigrants. It has rooms for seven persons.

76__Overtoom 197
The driving Dutchman

Today this building is occupied by the offices of car-hire companies, the usual suspects. There is little to reveal that the engine driving the motorisation of Dutch society once roared here.

The first car was seen in Holland in 1896, and 10 years later there were already 1,500 of them. Automobiles were a leisure activity for rich people in those days. They usually only travelled a short distance, and in the city, the maximum permitted speed was 10 kilometres per hour. Out in the country, a fabulous 15 kilometres per hour was allowed. Shortly before the outbreak of World War I there were several thousand cars in the Netherlands, and three young Amsterdamers came to the conclusion that this could be a market for the future. They founded the Reparatie Inrichting voor Automobielen (Automobile Repair and Installation Company; Riva for short), which moved into its branch on Overtoom in 1927.

These were the triumphal years of the motor car in Holland. Riva had the sales concession for the Ford T. This car, affordable for the middle class, was presented to a wide-eyed clientele in the premises on Overtoom, in a showroom that was impressive by the standards of the day. The workshops and the spare-part store were housed in the same building.

The founders of Riva surfed on a wave of success. They were admired and celebrated in the same way as start-up entrepreneurs today whose internet businesses are suddenly bought by big companies, making them billionaires. At Riva this role fell to the retail tycoon Albert Heijn, who became a majority shareholder. Soon the building on Overtoom was too small. Riva moved out to the surroundings of the city, and alongside Ford added other brands to the product range. But when you take a close look at the building today, on the façade you can still make out traces of the wonderful design of the old showroom.

Address Overtoom 197, NL-1054 HT Amsterdam (West) | **Getting there** Tram 7, 14 or 17 to Jan Pieter Heijestraat | **Hours** Viewable from the outside only | **Tip** Café Parck, Overtoom 458, is an amusing place and famous for its hamburgers.

77__Paradiso

Questions of faith in the world of music

In the 1960s, Paradiso represented what hippie circles of the time regarded as the true Amsterdam – even though, according to some reliable sources, it was often claimed that the building was no more than a church. Attitudes to the institution were definitely a matter of faith, and the owners played on its church associations. In the 1980s, for example, a swaying cross was placed on the roof.

Paradiso was founded in October 1967, shortly after the summer of love, and originated in a love-in that a few dozen hippies held in the nearby Vondel Park. They simply occupied the empty house and used it to carry on with their love-in. Back then, the place rejoiced in the name of the 'Cosmic Relaxation Center Paradiso'.

The presence of the squatters was legalised the following year. From then onwards, the house was considered a leisure centre, supported by a foundation, which gave its name to the building. From the very beginning, music had a big role in the programme. Performers at Paradiso included the early Pink Floyd, Captain Beefheart and Frank Zappa. Sometimes they are said to have played here for free, or in return for smokeable substances and other forms of payment in kind.

When the hippie era came to an end, Paradiso might well have closed down for ever, but it succeeded in making the transition to new times. Willem de Ridder, publisher of a pop magazine and the driving force behind the foundation of the place, took his leave in order to set up a pornographic magazine. He also tried to establish a sex academy in the city.

Paradiso carried on without him. The hippie temple turned itself into a bastion of the punk movement, and so it was able to continue. To this very day, probably every act in the western world that is worth its salt has played at Paradiso at least once. Half a million people a year swell the audience numbers, and the end is not in sight.

Address Weteringschans 6–8, NL-1017 SG Amsterdam (Centrum) | **Getting there**
Tram 1, 2 or 5 to Leidseplein | **Hours** Depend on programme, see www.paradiso.nl/
web/show | **Tip** De Melkweg (Milky Way) is another legendary address for pop music
(Lijnbaansgracht 234 A).

78__PIC

An insider's view

Years ago, the Red Light District of Amsterdam was an attraction that the city government actively used for advertising. The English band Police, in their early years, recorded the song *Roxanne* about a woman who works in the Red Light District. When George Michael produced his version of the song around the turn of the millennium, the video featured a local representative of the business, and the Dutch media reported in detail and approvingly on the fact. Today, however, the Amsterdam authorities are trying to change the character of the area – roughly speaking, the district between Zeedijk and Warmoesstraat. There are art initiatives, and efforts are being made to bring in fashion companies, to establish other hip projects, and to restrict the traditional red-light trade. However, the success of these endeavours is mixed.

Funds that were made available by the local government to convert to new purposes the houses with windows for sex workers were not called upon, and a hotline, introduced with a great deal of publicity, that prostitutes could call for help in emergencies was used exactly once in a whole quarter year.

In spite of all attempts to give it a new function, Amsterdam's Red Light District remains unique in the world in this form and concentration of activity. Some citizens think the new strategy for the area is going too far. One of them is Mariska Majoor, who runs the Prostitutie Informatie Centrum opposite the Oude Kerk. The name – abbreviated to PIC – has a double meaning: 'pik' is a Dutch slang word for the male organ. PIC provided information about the history of and conditions in the sex trade. Some critics think Mariska Majoor's view romanticises the subject, but no one can say she does not know what she is talking about. For a long time she published the trade journal *De Roode Draad* and before that she worked in the business herself.

Address Enge Kerksteeg 3, NL-1012 GV Amsterdam (Centrum) | **Getting there** Tram 4, 9, 16, 24 or 25 to Dam | **Hours** By arrangement, see www.pic-amsterdam.com | **Tip** Just round the corner on Oudekerksplein is a monument to Belle, an unknown prostitute. It was erected on the initiative of Mariska Majoor.

79__ The Polder House

One of the last of its kind

A polder – and please don't all pretend that you have always known this – is a piece of low-lying land for which the water levels within or around it can be regulated at will. This happens either by pumping water out or by damming it, and the details of this are possibly not all that complicated, and on the other hand not all that interesting either.

There are no fewer than 4,000 polders in the Netherlands. Half of all the polders in Europe are in Holland. You could therefore say with some justification that the Dutch are an absolute super-power when it comes to polders. For this reason Dutch hydraulic engineers were highly respected in Europe for centuries. Whether the task was to design fountains in France or to drain the fens in the east of England, usually Dutch engineers were called for and took on the job. As the saying goes, 'God created the world, but the Dutch created the Netherlands'.

A polder house is the home of the people who claimed the land from the sea. These dwellings were small and basic, and stood alone in the middle of meadows and pasture land. When their original occupants abandoned them, sometimes urban residents came along and used them as holiday homes.

As towns and cities expanded, incorporating the surrounding areas, the architecture changed. The polder houses disappeared, giving way to the typical gabled and canal-side houses. This house in the district of Pijp is an exception. It was built in 1865 in the style of polder houses because its modest dimensions meant that it was low-cost accommodation, even in the city. Perhaps the building was preserved because its occupants thought it was cute. Whatever the reason, it is one of only a few such houses that have not changed their character in the course of centuries. The current owners have given it a loving restoration using sustainable techniques.

Address Rustenburgerstraat 8, NL-1074 ET Amsterdam (Zuid) | Getting there Tram 3 to Amsteldijk | Hours Viewable from the outside only | Tip At Zeedijk 1 stands one of the last half-timbered houses in Amsterdam.

80_ The REM Island
Shiny happy people

This will be the last alphabetical riddle, and that's a promise. The REM island looks like a small oil rig. It's a house that stands in the water on stilts. It's conspicuous, and is meant to be so. REM stands for Reclame Exploitatie Maatschappij, i.e. advertising exploitation company. And that is exactly what it is. The owners wanted to run commercial radio and television stations. For this purpose, they had the house on stilts constructed at a shipyard in Ireland. From there, a tug pulled it to the North Sea, to a location just outside Dutch territorial waters, where TV Noordzee began to broadcast on 15 August, 1964.

At that time Dutch broadcasting laws did not allow private stations. From the official point of view this was a pirate broadcaster. It took a little time, but in November 1964 a law was passed prohibiting radio and TV on stilts. In December the Dutch navy confiscated all the equipment on the artificial island. This was only a partial success, however, as the authorities could do nothing to stop pirate stations from operating on ships.

These illegal beginnings on a platform later led, by indirect means, to the television station called TROS (for the sake of completeness: Televisie en Radio Omroep Stichting). Following its confiscation by the navy, the platform was used as a base for taking measurements of sea temperature and salt concentrations. By 2006 it had become too old, and was rusty. The building on the platform was cut away from the stilts and taken to Vlissingen. There it was purchased by a housing company that took it to its present location in Amsterdam, where it was placed on stilts once again and renovated.

Currently the REM island accommodates a restaurant, which can be hired to hold celebrations. So when the TROS television station had its 40th anniversary, of course there was only one place where the party could fittingly be held.

Address Haparandadam 45, NL-1013 AK Amsterdam (Centrum) | Getting there Bus 22, 48 or 348 to Oostzaanstraat | Hours Daily noon–10pm | Tip Okay, there's just one more little abbreviation: the ING Building (Amstelveenseweg 500) is thoroughly impressive, especially for its architecture.

81__The Rijksmuseum

A temple of art, not only for connoisseurs

The reopening of the Rijksmuseum was the other big event of 2013. To make sure that absolutely nothing went wrong, a rehearsal for every aspect of a museum visit (admission, cloakroom, circuit of the rooms, etc.) was held with students as test persons.

A few brief facts: the Rijksmuseum is the biggest museum in the Netherlands. It has 200 galleries and more than a million exhibits. Its best-known painting is – well, what do you think? – Rembrandt's *Nightwatch*.

The museum has had an eventful history. Its holdings have been under threat more than once. In the 19th century you could estimate extremely well the quality of a museum by looking at how many of its exhibits Napoleon carried off. In Amsterdam he took possession of quite a lot, but thanks to tough negotiations even before Waterloo, the Dutch were able to regain the items.

The collections survived World War II in a bunker in a hill near Maastricht. And one thing is possibly not well known: at Schiphol Airport there is a branch of the museum with a permanent exhibition of Dutch masters from the Golden Age, opened by Prince Willem Alexander, as he then was.

But I don't want to pretend that I have anything truly new to say about the Rijksmuseum. It's just that in a book with the title *111 Places that You Shouldn't Miss*, you can take a disrespectful attitude to almost any holy cow. However, in the case of the Rijksmuseum, the blasphemy would just be too shocking, so it could be said, quite simply: go and have a look, and overcome your inhibitions about high culture and your inertia. If you don't believe me, then browse a while on the website, where you can gain a good first impression of the collections. And if you still think the whole thing is too arty, then view the three 17th-century dolls' houses that the Rijksmuseum also owns. But go and have a look. Just go!

Address Museumstraat 1, NL-1071 XX Amsterdam (Zuid) | Getting there Tram 7, 10 to Spiegelgracht | Hours Daily 9am–5pm (last admission 4.30pm) | Tip The Van Gogh Museum just round the corner is also said to be good.

82__De Rode Hoed

Secrets for believers

Today 'the red hat' is an event venue. Debates and talk shows are held here. Everyone can come to say what they think and get it off their chest. If they think. But it was not always like this.

The building used to be occupied by a hat maker (hence the name). In 1629 the site was bought by the Remonstrants, a Protestant group, who turned the old hat workshop into a hidden church called the Vrijburg. When the Calvinists took power in Holland, in principle they declared freedom of thought, but not without adding a few explanatory nuances. Although freedom of conscience existed, which meant that anyone could pray to God as they wanted to, there was no freedom to hold church services in public. This right was reserved to the supporters of the religion that was dominant in the state.

But, to quote a man who ended up with an ice-pick in his skull on the orders of his mortal enemy, 'Religion is like a nail; the more you hit it, the deeper it goes.' Roman Catholics, Lutherans and Remonstrants wanted to be able to worship. They therefore built secret churches, which were not recognisable as such from outside, and met covertly to hold their services.

Of course, these efforts did not go unnoticed. The authorities reacted in different ways. Where in some towns it was forbidden for Catholics to move into adjacent houses (because the danger existed that they would secretly rip out the dividing walls and in this way convert the buildings into a room for worship), in other places a blind eye was turned – in return for a suitable financial contribution. And so there existed 'schuilkerken' (disguised churches), which from the inside could hardly be distinguished from normal, openly used churches.

The Vrijburg was used by the Remonstrants to hold services until 1957. This makes it the oldest surviving disguised church in the Netherlands, and it was certainly one of the largest.

Address Keizersgracht 102, NL-1015 CV Amsterdam (Centrum) | **Getting there** Tram 13, 14 or 17 to Westermarkt | **Hours** View from outside or hire a room: www.rodehoed.nl | **Tip** The Papegaai Kapel (Kalverstraat 58) also started out as a secret church.

83__RoXY

The house where house music began

The legend is roughly as follows: the year is 1987, the place is Ibiza. In the island's discotheques a new kind of music can suddenly be heard. With its monotone booming sound it drove everyone onto the dance floor, and even – something that was really new – got the boys to dance (instead of just watching the girls, as they did before).

When something makes such an impact in summer in the south, then all the sun-hungry north Europeans want the same thing at home. In London, the first house-music clubs were founded. And in Amsterdam it was RoXY, under the leadership of the artist Peter Giele.

The kick-off was sobering. An opening with the star Grace Jones, accompanied by lots of publicity, attracted the sum total of 34 paying guests. After a year, it seemed the organisers would have to throw in the towel, but thanks to solidarity and aid from London, the house trend got going in Amsterdam too.

The place filled up. Some DJs became famous. Celebrities were turned away or allowed inside, and all in all a lot of people had a lot of fun. The X and the Y in the name of the club were written in capital letters for a good reason. Along with hedonistic house music, the drug XTC (ecstasy) became fashionable, and at that time it was still legal.

Nevertheless, this new drug was a problem for the owners. Dealers were not the clientele that they dreamed of, so one of them went over to the police station in Warmoesstraat and asked the officers to cast an eye over their guests. Which they gladly did, but saw only happily writhing bodies and nothing illegal. Awareness of the problem came later, when ecstasy became a mainstream high. By that time, the drug was already out of fashion again at RoXY.

The club closed down after a fire in 1999. The fire broke out on the very day when the inspiration behind RoXY, Peter Giele, was buried. Some coincidences are simply legendary.

Address Singel 465, NL-1012 WP Amsterdam (Centrum) | Getting there Tram 4, 9, 16, 24 or 25 to Muntplein | Hours Viewable from the outside only | Tip If you like house music and visiting historic places, make a detour to Surinamekade, where the first Amsterdam open-air house party took place in 1988.

84 Ruigoord
Artists in residence?

After the Netherlands fought for and gained independence from Spain, things did not look too rosy for Catholics. Even when they dared to assemble and hold Mass, their churches were not allowed to be recognisable as such from the outside. They must have felt like the early Christians in Ancient Rome. Dutch Catholics later had the same position as the Irish in the British Empire. They were the underdogs, poorer than the others, with larger families. They often lived in their own villages.

Ruigoord was a typically Catholic place with its own church, and nothing much else – a rough place, which is what the name means. In the 1960s the village was scheduled for demolition, to make way for industry. Those were the days when high hopes were placed in oil, and the refineries in IJmuiden needed space to expand.

But this was, as already mentioned, back in the 1960s, and the evacuation of the village was greeted with protests, demonstrations and finally legal action. The conflict between politicians and citizens went on for years.

In the end, things were left to the lawyers, and – this is Holland after all – they found a compromise: on the one hand, the village was not to be wiped off the map (lengthy standing ovations from the residents), but on the other hand no one was to live there (contented smiles from politicians certain of their triumph).

Out of this state of limbo there developed the Ruigoord artists' colony, which sees itself as a sort of free-trade port for culture. It is a place of studios, workshops, performances, community events and festivals. The artistic activities that are initiated here radiate as far as the city centre of Amsterdam and have sparked off many an event there. Of course, if you ever should hear that the artists not only work but also somehow live in their studios and houses – well, that's no more than a rumour.

Address Stiftung Landjuweel, Ruigoord 76, NL-1047 HH Amsterdam (Westpoort) | **Getting there** By car: from the A10 ring road take the exit to the A5 towards Westpoort, then the first exit, Westpoortweg, until you see the Afrikahaven on the right | **Hours** Open all year, programme see www.ruigoord.nl | **Tip** Ruigoord was the inspiration for further events such as the Magneet Festival, held annually in late summer (www.magneetfestival.nl/en).

85 The Sarphati Monument

The man who cleaned things up

After the French occupation in Napoleon's time, Amsterdam fell into a deep slumber for two generations, and no one knew whether the city would ever wake up again. The unification of Germany in 1870–71 brought about a revival, as, thanks to some canal-building, Amsterdam became one of the largest ports for the German empire. Suddenly the city was growing again, and was in danger of acquiring all the problems that afflicted a metropolis like London or Berlin – slums, filth and epidemics, social misery. To prevent this, the doctor and reformer Samuel Sarphati organised housing associations, bakeries for cheap bread and a refuse collection system that really worked. Not everything that he tackled was a success (the Paleis voor Volksvlijt, based on the Crystal Palace in London, burned down quickly), and Sarphati died at the age of just 53.

Twenty years after his death, the city laid out Sarphati Park in his honour. Due to Amsterdam's problems with ground water it lies a little lower than the surrounding district and is enclosed by a metal fence, like many other parks in the city. The monument there was unveiled in 1886.

Under the German occupation, the park was renamed and the monument removed. You can guess the reason for this. The area around Sarphati Park was long considered a favourite address for local Bohemian society. Artists, writers and other would-be creative people moved in. Today, the district is especially popular among students.

The name Sarphati still stands for individualism. Amsterdam's first cycling street was recently installed next to Sarphati Park. It is very wide, the road surface is red, and the traffic lights are bike-friendly. This has had a positive effect on the behaviour of Amsterdam's cyclists, and so Sarphati Park is probably the only area where you can ride a bike in a relaxed manner, like in Copenhagen.

Address Sarphatipark, NL-1073 AA Amsterdam (Zuid/De Pijp) | Getting there Tram 3 to 2e van der Helststraat | Tip Frederiksplein is close by. This square gives an idea of how imposing the Paleis voor Volksvlijt must once have seemed. The buildings of the Nederlandsche Bank that now stand here are less impressive.

86 Schiffmacher & Veldhoen Tattooing

Bye-bye tramp stamp

Henk Schiffmacher (who incidentally is also known as 'Hanky Panky'), is a legend. He has seen them all. Kurt Cobain. The Red Hot Chili Peppers. The boys from Pearl Jam. Lemmy from Motörhead. Herman Brood, of course. And many, many others. They have all been to him to have a tattoo made. His establishment has a reputation as one of the best tattoo studios in the world, and there are good reasons to think that this is right. The mere sight of the illustrations on the walls shows that they are far away from the world of the 'tramp stamp'.

Henk Schiffmacher was never very interested in anything they tried to teach him at school. He came from a family of butchers, and originally wanted to become a painter. And he still does. He also travels around the world, collects exhibits (as long as they are connected to tattooing), gives lectures and ensures that his art and his *oeuvre* are treated with the respect they deserve. Some people think that his work has had the effect of removing tattooing from the dubious niche it occupied and making it part of mainstream culture.

Tattooing has the status of an ancient craft for Henk Schiffmacher. A craft in which know-how is passed on in the traditional manner from the master to apprentices, who then become journeymen and masters themselves. The story is told that tattooers first practise on themselves, and then on pieces of pork. That may be, but Henk Schiffmacher is not the kind of person of whom you would ask a question like that. He has not only beautified the bodies of other people, he is a walking work of art himself, and has taken on Tycho Veldhoen as a partner in the business. His daughter Morrison also works in the studio.

The designs most in demand are still the classics. First of all, wise or less wise sayings. Second: pin-ups, roses and anchors. Third: birds. Fourth: names.

Address Ceintuurbaan 416, NL-1074 EA Amsterdam (Zuid) | Getting there Tram 3 or 25 to Ceintuurbaan/Van Woustraat | Hours Tue–Sun 11am–7pm, but it is advisable to make an appointment: +31 (20)4705578, www.tattooing.nl | Tip Also blue, like most tattoos, but less painful: Delft Blue. These famous tiles can be seen at Muntplein 12.

87 __ The Shipyard

Just carry on

The city's big shipyards all had their days of greatness and eventually experienced their demise. But one small-scale ship-builder has out-lived them all.

In 1625 Peter Minuit set out for America on behalf of the Dutch West India Company. Having landed there, he negotiated with the Native Americans about an island called 'Manna-hata', which he finally purchased for 60 guilders. The rest, as they say, is history.

Two years after the departure of his ship, the first vessel went onto the slipway at the shipyard, which is family-owned today. Over the centuries, ships were built here that crossed the world and sailed the seven seas.

In 1885 the Bierenbroodspot family took over the business. After this acquisition, the company stayed the way it had always been: small, compact, family-run. And this strategy has enabled it to survive to the present day. The shipyard is the oldest in the Netherlands.

Many of the old dockland sites in this neighbourhood have been converted to new uses, but this shipyard has stayed true to its history. This does not, however, mean that these shipbuilders are not open to modern developments.

Recently, the shipbuilding hall was roofed over so that in future the employees will have better protection against the wind and the elements as they work. It is reported that this epoch-making innovation was greeted by the workforce with delight and satisfaction.

All those who are interested can form their own impression of what it is like to work in a piece of industrial heritage. Provided that the boss is on site and has time for visitors. And provided that work is going on. Out of consideration for the neighbours, the company does not start work in the morning until half past eight, and at four o'clock in the afternoon the workers already down tools for the day.

Address Vierwindenstraat 10, NL-1013 LA Amsterdam (Centrum) | Getting there
Tram 3 to Zoutkeetsgracht | Hours Viewable from the outside only | Tip On a rainy
day the Scheepvaartmuseum (Kattenburgerplein 1) is hard to beat.

88__The Smoker's Seminar
High school

Let's assume you really came to Amsterdam to enjoy the arts or the history, or because of the flowers. Or the cheese. And then, as you walk around the city you notice a sweetish aroma, often emanating from foolish tourists who wink conspiratorially at the locals, and are often rewarded with an amused lack of sympathy – plenty of Dutch people will convincingly explain that hardly anything tempts them less than smoking a joint. That's how it is with many prohibitions. When something is no longer banned, its attraction disappears. And when you see this repeatedly, your urge to research is awakened. Now you could, purely out of academic interest of course, take a seat in one of those coffee shops, but what happens when you look at the menu and realise that it might as well have been written in Ancient Greek? Not to mention all the refinements of rolling your joint, etc.?

For interested persons of this kind, AllTourNative holds a so-called smoker's seminar, specially aimed at people who don't want to fry their brains but simply wish to know what it is all about. After that, they can all decide for themselves how many of their opinions were prejudices.

The teacher, of whom it is known only that she is in her mid-thirties and comes from the Middle East, naturally has such a lead in knowledge, thanks to her place of origin, that participants can hardly hope to catch up with her. Yet, to say it again: how far theory becomes practice in this seminar is a matter for everyone himself or herself to decide. Those who only want to roll up (no pun intended) and try it are just as welcome as regular users whose aim is to perfect their technique. In any case, everyone who keeps a clear head for long enough will learn about the cultivation, origin and processing of the smokeable goods that stimulate the imagination of so many visitors to Amsterdam.

Address AllTourNative, Johan Huizingalaan 87–89 HS, NL-1065, HW Amsterdam (Nieuw West); the seminar venue is announced after registration | Getting there Bus 18, 64 or 353 to Robert Fruinlaan | Hours Information: www.alltournative-amsterdam.com/tours/smoking-workshop (1.5 hrs) or +31 (6)24990721 | Tip The Hash Marihuana & Hemp Museum (Oudezijds Achterburgwal 148) is for people who want to study the matter in depth.

89 The Spectacles Museum
Clear-sighted for centuries

Antoni van Leeuwenhoek was a wise man who lived in the 17th century. He was a naturalist, land surveyor, a researcher and a scholar with many interests who became famous for two things above all: his first, home-made microscope and something that he examined under this microscope.

Microscopes already existed before Leeuweenhoek turned his attention to the subject, but they had a modest power of magnification. Antoni van Leeuweenhoek was not satisfied with a mere 30-fold enlargement. His microscopes, which he designed and made himself and fitted with lenses for which he had personally ground the glass, easily achieved more than 10 times this magnification.

This, of course, had consequences. While his English competitors were looking at fleas and other small creatures through their lenses and describing them, Leeuweenhoek searched for items to investigate that would demonstrate the impressive performance of his own device. He found a suitable object of study among the male bodily fluids. No, it was not saliva. And yes, a boy in puberty would probably have hit on the same idea.

When you then also consider that Leeuwenhoek was not the only one to make pioneering discoveries in the field of optics in the Netherlands, then it comes as no surprise to find a museum of spectacles in Amsterdam that presents seven centuries of the history of eye-glasses in a knowledgeable and loving way. Here the well-known phrase 'hands-on display' is taken seriously. This quirky museum not only exhibits spectacles from the past. If you would like to do so, in the museum shop you can also buy a historic-looking model. Whatever look you aspire to, from Buddy Holly or John Lennon to one of the great classical composers that the world has brought forth – here you will find a pair of glasses to your taste (and modern varieties, too, it goes without saying).

Address Gasthuismolensteeg 7, NL-1017 AM Amsterdam (Centrum) | **Getting there** Tram 1, 2 or 5 to Dam/Paleisstraat | **Hours** Wed–Fri 11.30am–5.30pm, Sat 11.30am–5pm | **Tip** The museum is situated in a small quarter called Negen Straatjes, an especially picturesque part of Amsterdam.

90___The Spinoza Monument
The task of the state is to defend freedom

Baruch Spinoza was a 17th-century Dutch philosopher whose supporters found his view of the world clear and focused. This may have had something to do with the fact that he worked as a lens grinder. He was a contemporary of Descartes and Leibniz, who visited him to discuss the migration of souls. Spinoza was best known for his posthumously published *Ethics*, which expresses its principles independently of theological norms and can therefore be interpreted across all religions. According to this, the state should not prescribe what its citizens should do but ensure that each of them can develop.

In his lifetime Spinoza, considered by many to be the greatest thinker of his age, was both attacked and honoured, and this continued after this death. Einstein admired him and the highest-ranking Dutch scientific prize was named after him. His portrait adorned the old thousand-guilder note. On the other hand, Christian schools wanted to remove him from the syllabus at the same time as he was included in the canon of Dutch thinkers.

In 2008 Spinoza's statue was unveiled. It stands directly below the office of the mayor, who – if he wants – can glance at it every day, for every decision and every measure. The reason for the erection of the monument was the eternal rivalry between the cities of Amsterdam and Rotterdam. In Rotterdam there was a statue of Erasmus, so Amsterdam just had to have one of Spinoza. A further, more important reason lay in contemporary events. Spinoza's parents were Jewish immigrants who had fled from Portugal to the Netherlands, and were taken in here regardless of all religious and cultural differences. The monument emphasises that this tradition should not be forgotten in Amsterdam. The rose-ringed parakeets that ornament the statue represent birds that have flown to the city from other climates and have now become acclimatised in Vondel Park.

Address Zwanenburgwal, NL-1011 JH Amsterdam (Centrum) | Getting there Metro 51, 53 or 54 to Waterlooplein | Tip The Pinto House at Sint Antoniesbreestraat 69 belonged to a Jewish family that fled from Portugal at the time when Spinoza was active in Amsterdam.

91 __ The Storks' Nest

Flying high over the park

Frankendael Park is a well-known name in Amsterdam. It is the site of the last remaining fine country house within the city boundaries. All the others have been swallowed up by the city in the course of its never-ending expansion.

In 1629 the Dutch once again celebrated a great triumph of land over water. A lake area called the Watergrafsmeer was reclaimed and made into a polder. (Here a linguistic footnote: the Dutch refer to the sea or ocean as 'de zee', whereas a lake is called 'het meer', like the English word 'mere'.)

This newly gained land was in great demand, and therefore was divided up into plots for 40 residences. The sole house that has remained standing until the present day was built in 1695, and it is impossible to overlook the fact that the French Sun King Louis XIV was the supreme trendsetter at that time. Many aspects of the park and the house have a whiff of 'little Versailles' about them.

In the green expanse of the park, covering an area of seven hectares, a marble fountain splashes. Nearby, a tree nursery and a greenhouse can be seen. And all of this splendour is actually subterranean, in a sense: Watergraafsmeer lies some six metres below sea level. Everyone who arrives here has reached the lowest point in Amsterdam.

And now we come to the main point. This architectural magnificence and beautiful landscape gardening are all very well. The lawns and the gravel-strewn paths, as well as the huge, centuries-old trees, are very fine. But what really captivates visitors in Frankendael Park is a pair of storks that in the last few years have regularly nested on top of the chimney of a former factory.

The excitement reaches its peak when the young storks have hatched and it is time for them to learn to fly. It has even been necessary to call in the fire brigade when overenthusiastic young storks fell out of the nest.

Address Park Frankendael, NL-1097 Amsterdam (Zuidoost/Watergraafsmeer) | Getting there Tram 9 to Hugo de Vrieslaan | Hours House by arrangement, see www.park-frankendael.nl | Tip Zon's Hofje (Prinsengracht 159) is another green idyll, open daily 10am–5pm. Please consider the local residents!

92 The Student Containers
Does it stack up?

Students are the subjects of as many clichés as the Netherlands. Lots of time, not much money – yet everyone now says that things used to be different. Whatever the truth of these beliefs, for the foreseeable future there is one proven fact: affordable accommodation for students is as rare and as sought-after in Amsterdam as in other cities.

As a means of mitigating this problem, if not actually solving it, 380 shipping containers were put ashore at the harbour and converted into student flats.

As an architectural practice was behind this project, the containers were not simply dumped in the port, but arranged to form an aesthetically interesting ensemble. Every one of the containers, which are coloured red, orange, blue and white (these happen to be the colours of the Dutch national flag and the emblematic colour of the royal house of Orange), was made into a small apartment. Each of them has a size of 24 square metres, and is equipped with a kitchen, shower and toilet.

Originally the whole project was planned as a temporary measure. The intention was that, after a while, the containers would be transported to the south of the city, as further plans had been made for the harbour district, and the container village was only for the interim period. However, the containers were so popular, that they were left in place. In the meantime, other cities in Europe have taken up this original way of providing living space.

As things stand, all concerned are satisfied. The students are pleased to have low-cost accommodation. The harbour district has lost some of its post-industrial bleakness by gaining new residents.

It can only be hoped that living a student's life in standardised, stackable boxes does no damage to individual development. If this method of storage for young people results in graduates who cannot think outside the box, the efforts will have been in vain.

Address Stavangerweg 50–877 AT & Gevleweg 20–91 AX & Ms. Oslofjordweg 557,
NL-1033 SL Amsterdam (Noord) | Getting there Bus 391 or 394 to Stenendokweg |
Hours Viewable from the outside only | Tip The restaurant boat Pollux is nearby at
M. T. Ondinaweg, Pier 12.

93__Surfcenter IJburg

Wild water adventures in the city

To be honest, most people are happy when it doesn't rain. But just assuming that the sun shines for an extended period, and you don't feel like going to all the usual places, and, for heaven's sake, Amsterdam is a port city after all, then it ought to be possible to have a good time on the water, doing water sports. And by that, I don't mean just sitting on the beach and looking out to sea.

For those who always wanted to learn how to skid across the water on a windsurfing board, or at least to try it out, Surfcenter Ijburg is the right place to go.

Frank van Zwieten is a true professional. Before he opened his windsurfing centre in Amsterdam he worked in Florida. And you can tell that he has some talent as a teacher from the fact that he even taught his own son how to windsurf. And the son is now employed abroad, initiating new disciples into the art of standing on a board with a sail. It is rumoured that van Zwieten's offspring is now even better at the sport than his father, who keeps his cool when this is suggested. What's important to him is that those who come to him enjoy the sport and can practise it at the level of achievement that is right for them.

The advantage of IJburg as a place for windsurfing is that you can get there by tram in little more than 15 minutes, yet the site and the facilities there are perfectly comparable with some places that are right by the sea.

The surface of water available to windsurfers is miles wide here, and there is no lack of wind. One thing that makes the sport more attractive to beginners than it was in the past is that a lot of progress has been made with the materials and equipment. Everything has become simpler, literally. You can now even go windsurfing on an inflatable board. But to find out how that works, it is better to ask the experts. And you will find plenty of them at Surfcenter IJburg.

Address Corner of Bert Haanstrakade and Pampuslaan, NL-1087 HN Amsterdam (IJburg) | Getting there Tram 26 to IJburg | Hours Sat & Sun 11am–6pm, in the high season also Wed & Fri 2–9pm, Thu 6–9pm: for information, see www.surfcenterijburg.nl | Tip By Amsterdam's standards, the nature reserve De Oeverlanden on the Nieuwe Meer is quite wild.

94__De Taart van m'n Tante

When the tart is art

The brains behind this company (the name means 'my aunt's tart') are two young men who have obviously set themselves several aims. First, to create cakes and other pastries that are almost too beautiful to eat. Second, to turn the sale and presentation of these works of art into big events, at which such a song and dance is made about the cake, with such interest on the part of the public and media, that you wonder if they can really still be eaten when it is all over. And, finally, the aim of their methods of production must also be to lend to pastry cooks the aura of true artists.

If this was the master plan, then you have to acknowledge that every point has been fulfilled. Simon De Jong and Noam Offer are celebrated on all sides as the rising stars in the pastry-cook firmament. Their masterpieces of the baker's art are of course consumed at weddings and birthdays, but they are also engaged more and more often by companies who want to give their employees a treat after months of slave labour.

The roll call of prominent Dutch people for whom De Jong and Offer have kneaded dough is impressively long: Johan Cruijff, the former prime minister Wim Kok, and members of the royal family have all graced the customer list.

It will surely not be very long before the way to recognise a BN ('bekende Nederlander', the local expression for an A, B or C-list celebrity) is that he or she has been honoured with a celebration organised by De Taart van m'n Tante.

It goes without saying that all this fuss quickly attracted the film and television people. The two 'taartists' have already supplied pastries for several productions, and even played a leading role in some of them. Foreign television channels have also noticed, and broadcast reports on the company. It is only a matter of time before they are world-famous. That would be the icing on the cake.

Address Ferdinand Bolstraat 10, NL-1072 LJ Amsterdam (Oud Pijp) | **Getting there** Tram 16 or 24 to Stadhouderskade | **Hours** Daily 10am–6pm | **Tip** While we are on the subject of eating: the gourmet restaurant D'Vijff Vlieghen (The Five Flies) in Spuistraat is the best in town. Don't be put off by the name.

95 Tassenmuseum Hendrikje
Bags of historic fun

Whether it is a mark of divine irony that in Amsterdam of all places, a city that is notorious for pickpockets, there should be a museum devoted to bags – well, you can decide that for yourself. But the fact remains that this is the only museum about which locals have told me either that they have already paid a visit or that they will definitely go – for the first or second time.

The collection of Tassenmuseum Hendrikje – The Museum of Bags and Purses – contains 4,000 handbags, the oldest dating from about 1600. The presiding spirit of the museum was Hendrikje Ivo, who discovered her love of handbags when a particularly high-class example, made in 1820, fell into her hands. That, at least, is the official version of the story. In my experience, however, a love of handbags is indelibly written into the genetic code of many women, and they need no eureka moment of any kind to discover this affinity.

Everything in the museum revolves around bags. You can learn how they are manufactured, about their materials, shapes and colours. And if you really want to educate yourself in the subject, in the museum shop you can buy a book about the history of the handbag. When you have closely studied all 500 illustrations in the work, you ought to be considered an expert.

Of course, you can buy bags as part of your visit. The items on sale are designer products, not exhibits from the museum collections. And if you have something special at home that you would like to donate to the museum, then the people who run it will be pleased to hear from you.

What started out as a passion for collecting on the part of one individual has now grown into a proper organisation with curators, board members and specialist advisers. And though the emphasis of this museum is on the pleasure to be had from bags, it should not be thought of as merely some kind of joke.

Address Herengracht 573, NL-1017 CD Amsterdam (Centrum) | Getting there Tram 4, 7, 9 or 14 to Rembrandtplein | Hours Daily 10am–5pm | Tip Men who get bored here can go to the Pijpenkabinet (Prinsengracht 488), a collection of over 20,000 pipes.

96_ The Torpedo Theatre

Drama, texts and a quiet voice

Torpedo is an old Dutch brand of portable typewriters for travellers. The name was adopted by a small, high-class literary magazine that was printed by various publishing houses at irregular intervals, but unfortunately never acquired the large readership that it deserved. If a publication is neither pretentiously literary nor simply noisy and gaudy, the world is not kind to it.

As the people who produced *Torpedo* wanted their texts and ideas to reach the public regardless of this, they turned their magazine into the Torpedo Theatre. According to the advertising, it is Amsterdam's smallest theatre, which is absolutely believable when you know that the venue was once home to a puppet theatre. The original stage was no larger than the small round windows through which tickets used to be sold at railway stations.

The prevailing atmosphere on the premises is sociable and friendly, and is enjoyable even if you do not speak Dutch and have no interest in literary entertainment. The main purpose of going to the Torpedo Theatre is to have fun and spend some time together pleasantly. Which is why, although it has not taken first place in any theatre rankings so far, it has come out top in a survey to find the cosiest pub.

The events include performances by singer-songwriters, which match the surroundings well, evenings devoted to specific countries, information on a theme 'from both ends of the sausage' (no, that isn't meant to be taken seriously), and some truly off-the-wall shows, as when a Dutchman called Friedrich Hlawatsch took the stage to sing well-known hits that he had laboriously translated from Dutch into German. It was amusing and well worth hearing. Carel Helder, the main man behind the literary magazine, was quick to appreciate the opportunities that arise for a high-quality publication when it opens its own performance venue.

Address Sint Pieterspoortsteeg 33, NL-1012 HM Amsterdam (Centrum) | Getting there Tram 4, 9, 16, 24, 25 or 26 to Dam | Hours During performances; see www.torpedotheater.nl | Tip Nes, a street of many theatres, is just round the corner.

97___The Tsar's Residence

Where Peter the Russian had great parties

There are many and diverse connections between the Netherlands and Russia. A vodka museum that opened not long ago at Damrak has already closed again, but the Hermitage in St Petersburg has a branch in the city, which is to be found in the former Amstelhof. And then, of course, there is Tsar Peter the Great, who visited Amsterdam at the end of the 17th century.

Peter the Great was a trendsetter in a number of ways. For one thing, he was one of the few monarchs named 'the Great' who was indeed also big (he was 2.04 metres tall), and he was also the first tsar to make an appearance in western Europe.

After staying for a few years, he returned to Russia and transferred the capital of his empire from Moscow to St Petersburg, where a number of influences from Amsterdam were evident in the urban planning. Like Amsterdam, St Petersburg consists of a series of small islands, which are all linked by more than 500 bridges.

Peter the Great loved ships and yachts. Of course, Amsterdam was the perfect place for him, as the Dutch were the leading maritime nation in that period. The tsar was initiated into the secrets of ship-building during his stay in the city, and he joined in the work himself.

It is also reported that His Majesty not only worked in the shipyards (under the pseudonym of Pjotr Mikhailov – but that didn't really fool anyone), but was well able to enjoy some entertainment. Contemporaries reported that a large royal person could often be seen swaying from side to side as he approached the house on Keizersgracht where many a party is said to have taken place.

Some people even believe that the Dutch national flag (red, white and blue) inspired an intoxicated Peter to choose the Russian national colours (white, blue and red). It is doubtful whether this is true, but it is at least a nice story – because the two flags can easily be confused, even today.

Address Keizersgracht 317, NL-1016 EE Amsterdam (Centrum/Jordaan) | Getting there Tram 1, 2 or 5 to Spui | Hours Viewable from the outside only | Tip The Hermitage (Amstel 51) is a branch of the famous gallery in St Petersburg. It has an exhibition about Peter the Great.

98__ Twilight Tours

Amsterdam after dark

Every city has its darker aspects, which can be appreciated best by taking a tour at night. Then you can go to places where terrible things happened in bygone centuries.

There are ghosts from the past that don't want to leave us in peace and can only be laid to rest when they have passed on their legacy to us, who come after them.

The actor and singer Tessa Hoss, who knows the history and contexts of her city as few others, decided a few years ago to create a programme that intermingles the crimes and circumstances of past times with other urban myths. Her intention was to communicate the background to the places visited, for people who did not know the locations, by means of songs, ballads and fables. It is an integral part of her plan that the performance should not be without some strange and creepy effects.

Her means of transport is an old American road cruiser, a Chevrolet Caprice, which of course has its own life story. This huge vehicle was once used as a hearse. Those who are willing to accept on its own terms the style of this night-time show can learn much more in one and a half hours, while the performer tells her stories in the car and acts out scenes from the scary side of Amsterdam's history at carefully chosen sites, than could be gathered from any book or museum. It is almost as if you were sitting in a ghost train, except that the stage sets are not from a theatre, but places in the real-life city of Amsterdam.

The old Chevrolet is extremely well-suited for playing out dramatic scenes. It was not part of the original plan, as the intention was to hold the tour in a bus, which would have provided more space for performers and audience. However, the bus driver was killed in a traffic accident and the bus was damaged beyond repair. (And that is a serious, true story.)

Address Silodam 7, NL-1013 AL Amsterdam (Centrum) | Getting there Bus 48 to
Barentszplein | Hours Tours, also in English by arrangement: www.blondenblauw.nl | Tip
A more commercial attraction to send a shiver down your spine: the Amsterdam Dungeon
at Rokin 78 has the usual horrors.

99__Typically Dutch
In costume

I don't know if there is really a demand for this, but I would like to point out that the opportunity exists. In Volendam, a village near Amsterdam – once just as Catholic as Ruigoord – you can have your photograph taken wearing authentic traditional Dutch costume.

In principle, we know two things about Dutch costume. We think we have seen more than enough of the women's version. As far as the male costume is concerned, many people don't even know it exists. The reason for this is the advertising figure called Antje, with her bonnet, dress and fixed smile, who has been used for decades to sell cheese, cheese, and even more cheese. It would be wrong to think her clothing is typical for Holland. But it is indeed typical for Volendam.

The men's dress looks exactly the same, except that the skirts are shorter. No, seriously: here, as everywhere else, folk costume derives from the clothes worn for work. Many families in Volendam got their livelihood from fishing, and this influenced the clothes they wore (for example, boots into which they could stuff their trouser legs).

The De Boer photo studio is situated right by the dike, and the tradition of taking photographs of guests wearing traditional costume has been going a long time. As far back as the 1920s, Pouw de Boer noticed that American tourists were delighted to swap clothes with the locals. This gave him the idea of organising the whole thing professionally in a photographer's studio.

It was a good idea. Over many years thousands of tourists have had their photos taken, and the business has now been taken over by Pouw's grandchildren. The shots are taken inside the shop, where customers can choose between three different backdrops: the harbour, the home or a neutral scene. This may not look as authentic as a photo taken in the open air, but the advantage is that you can do it in all weathers.

Address Haven 82, NL-1131 ET Volendam | Getting there Bus 118 to Volendam | Hours Daily 9am–6pm; bookings are not necessary but possible; for information +31 (299)363607 or www.fotoinvolendamkostuum.nl | Tip If you go by car, you can drive from Volendam to nearby Waterland.

100__ The Valckenier House

Soul striptease for the trendy

A group of tourists has booked a guided tour of the Red Light District. Looking slightly stunned, the group staggers towards the last stop on its educational walk. Moderately interested, the participants learn that they are now standing in front of the house of the Valckenier family, a major dynasty of Amsterdam merchants who made their fortune from the trade in salted cod. Their interest becomes even more moderate and their eyes wander away from the guide.

Not even the information that the structural framework of the building dates from 1492, the year when Columbus set off for America, can really arouse their enthusiasm.

'As you see, this is the only house with its own landing stage. This tells us a lot about the importance of the family', says the tour guide.

'Yes, all right. Very good. Have we finished now?' 'Nearly', says the guide, to general disappointment. All these historical details are no doubt important and instructive, but ... after all, we are in Amsterdam, aren't we? And then the tour guide smiles and adds 'Actually I wanted to tell you something about the striptease courses that are held in this house.'

Suddenly he has their undivided attention. This is more like it.

'The courses are organised by Rob van Hulst (see photo), a Dutch actor, entrepreneur and all-round celebrity. They are carried out by a blonde hotel heiress.'

Blonde? Hotel heiress? 'Surely that can't be...'

'No, not Paris Hilton. You could say that she is better-looking. And knows more. There's nothing seedy about this at all. It's about self-confidence and awareness of your body. You learn to take off your clothes without laying bare your soul.'

The listeners in the group are extremely interested, and the mood has become lighter. One digs his neighbour in the ribs: 'There you are! It was a good idea after all to book this historical tour.'

Address Oudezijds Voorburgwal 57, NL-1012 EJ Amsterdam (Centrum) | **Getting there** Tram 4, 9, 16, 24, 25 or 26 to Dam | **Hours** For information about the programme, see www.robvanhulst.nl | **Tip** Further themed tours are run by Get Events (www.getevents.nl).

101__ Vondel Park

A green space with the work of a genius

Joost van den Vondel was one of the great Dutch poets. Born in Shakespeare's time, he wrote plays and polemical poetry that must have made his contemporaries extremely angry. His best-known play is called *Gijsbrecht van Aemstel*, and the others are even less well-known (the 'e' following the 'A' in Aemstel is not pronounced, being merely an archaic Dutch spelling). Vondel often got into trouble with the clergy, and the biting satire of his works only becomes clear to us nowadays if we study them closely and have the appropriate secondary literature at hand for reference.

Vondel Park is the largest green space in Amsterdam. This fact may not be particularly impressive, as the city is not blessed with many large parks, but one of them has to hold the title, and the park does this job very well.

Needless to say, what happens here is what happens in all parks all over the world. Apart from riding bicycles, picnicking and taking their dogs for a walk, some people go into the bushes and – well, they copulate. However, Vondel Park is probably the one park in the world that has produced rules for this practice. Really, truly: it has been officially laid down that sexual contact many only take place after dusk, out of sight to children, and not on playgrounds. Condoms and other accessories may not be left behind at the spots where the activity took place.

You might think that 90 per cent of these regulations are a matter of plain common sense, but the authorities believe that by issuing these rules, they have helped to restrict the frequency of sexual congress in the park.

In 1965 Vondel Park celebrated its 100th anniversary. On this occasion an art exhibition was held, and a world-famous artist was involved: Picasso. When the exhibition came to an end, he donated his exhibit to the city of Amsterdam, since when the park has possessed a fish by Picasso.

Address Museumkwartier, NL-1054 Amsterdam (Oud Zuid) | Getting there Tram 3 or 12 to Van Baerlestraat | Hours Open 24 hours | Tip The Cobra Museum of Modern Art (Sandbergplein 1, NL-1181 ZX Amstelveen) has moved out of the city centre and is therefore often overlooked. Unjustly.

102__ The Water Taxi

Water trips for all

Amsterdam's taxis do not have a great reputation. Repeatedly there have been stories in the media about taxi drivers who refused to take a blind person's guide-dog or who cheated tourists. This may be little consolation for visitors from abroad, but even native Dutch people have reported that Amsterdam taxi drivers, as soon as they heard a dialect from outside the city, have taken them on a round trip that they never asked for. There is, however, a fairly reliable way of turning a journey by taxi into an experience that you will always remember with pleasure: the water taxi.

The water taxis are operated by a company that also navigates sightseeing boats around the canals. The advantage of this is that they know how to get around on the waterways. The design of boats is based on that of New York's famous yellow cabs, and they have seats for up to eight persons. You can order a water taxi by telephone, just like a four-wheeled one, and it will pick you up at the agreed place.

Of course you can use a water taxi to get from A to B in the normal manner, but it is also possible to agree with the driver (is it right to say 'driver' for the man who steers a water taxi, or should we call him the captain? – I have no idea, to be honest) on an individual tour of the city, passing only the sights that you are really interested in.

And if you would like your trip to be even more special, you can book a VIP water taxi. These versions are not painted bright yellow, but a more restrained charcoal grey, and the way passengers are treated on board differs from the style of a normal taxi journey more or less in the same way as economy class differs from business class on an aircraft. During the tour around the canals through 'the biggest open-air museum in the Netherlands', passengers are treated to snacks and drinks, and if that is not enough, there is even a mini-bar.

Address Prins Hendrikkade 25, NL-1012 TM Amsterdam (Centrum) | Getting there Centraal Station | Hours Information: www.water-taxi.nl or +31 (20)5356363 | Tip Insiders recommend dawn as the time for a canal trip, when the last night owls are going to bed and the sun starts to wake the city.

103__Wertheim Park

A haven of peace

Amsterdam is a noisy city – let's not try to pretend otherwise. There is always someone making a din. Honking horns, roaring, beating, rattling, shouting, crashing, clinking and then that monotonous peep-peep-peep, where you get the impression that the whole city is manoeuvring backwards into a parking space. It can't be a coincidence that the glockenspiel was invented here, as well as its sadistic distant relative, the dreadful, droning barrel organ.

The locals take a stoical attitude to the noise: if you can't stand it, don't come here. But of course, even the acoustically hardened residents of Amsterdam need phases of tranquillity. Those who live in the canal district and can afford to do so retreat to their country homes in Hoge Veluwe in Overijssel province when it all gets too much.

But there are a few havens of peace and quiet in the city. So many of them, to be honest, that it's hard to make a choice. Funenpark, the Begijnhof and the Harmoniehof are all quiet spots, and the park of the Institut Français is also very attractive, though unfortunately only accessible by arrangement. So in the end we will opt for Wertheim Park, because it is the only large park in the Centrum district.

Wertheim Park is easy to reach and has an impressive gateway. As soon as you have passed through this entrance, you seem to have come to a different world. If there was not so much litter, you would think you were out in the country.

The sights in the park include a big fountain and the Auschwitz Monument, erected in 1993. The park takes its name from the Jewish philanthropist and banker Abraham Carel Wertheim. On 14 August, 1942, during the German occupation, the mayor of Amsterdam decided that this name was no longer in keeping with the times, and until the end of the war, a different name was in used: Tuinpark (garden park). In 1945 the old name was rightfully reinstated.

Address Plantage Middenlaan 1, NL-1018 DA Amsterdam (Centrum) | **Getting there**
Tram 4 or 19 to Plantage Kerklaan | **Hours** Daily 7am–9pm | **Tip** A different way to do it:
Club 8 (Admiraal de Ruijterweg 56B) puts on silent disco events, where everyone listens to
the music from their own headset, and otherwise it is quiet.

104__ The Westergasfabriek
Industrial heritage and media

The Westergasfabriek was constructed in 1883 by the British Imperial Continental Gas Association. On completion it was the largest municipal utility in Amsterdam. The gas produced from coal was used in the city until Dutch natural gas was found in the 1960s in Slochteren, in the north of the Netherlands, and a country that is poor in natural resources became a little less dependent on imports.

There seem to be decommissioned gasometers in every big European city, and the same idea is clearly in fashion everywhere: the setting and atmosphere are so powerful that you simply have to turn the site into a park for the arts. But what makes this place attractive to visitors is that they can, if they want, get involved in the leisure life of Amsterdam away from all the tourist hustle and bustle. On the site of the Westergasfabriek you can do what people do in other parks (relax, have a stroll, et cetera), and there are also lots of cultural activities. Several times a year, huge open-air concerts take place.

I would have been delighted to report that the Westergasfabriek is distinguished from other gasometers by its fine qualities, and that no hot air is produced here in talk shows and the like, but unfortunately this is not true. A television show is made on the premises of the Westergasfabriek: *De Wereld Draait Door*. This is an ambiguous title, as it can be understood on the one hand as 'The World Keeps on Turning' and on the other hand as 'The World Is a Crazy Place'.

Of course tickets for this show are in great demand, and it goes without saying that you can look into the studio while the programme is being recorded. But that is one of the advantages of being abroad: you are as indifferent to all the hype about local celebrities as you probably ought to be at home. Because real life happens outside the doors of the studio. In the Westergasfabriek, for example.

Address Polonceaukade 23, NL-1014 DA Amsterdam (Westpoort) | **Getting there** Bus 348 to Van Limburg Stirumstraat | **Hours** For information about the programme, see www.westergasfabriek.nl | **Tip** On this site is a rock 'n' roll pub called Pacific Parc. Its self-service outdoor terrace is a great place to hang out in summer.

105__ The WG Site

Winter pleasures on the ski slopes

'WG' stands for 'Wilhelmina Gasthuis'. And 'Gasthuis' here does not mean a guesthouse, but a hospital, and in the past often a psychiatric institution.

For a long time the Wilhelmina Gasthuis was the biggest hospital in the city. It took its name from the fact that the ten-year-old Queen Wilhelmina (the great-grandmother of the present reigning monarch, King Willem-Alexander) laid the foundation stone in 1891.

The Wilhelmina Gasthuis grew and grew. At one time it accommodated 1,700 beds in 20 wards, as well as a school for nurses. But the day came when even this was not enough. In 1980 a new university clinic, the AMC (Academisch Medisch Centrum), was opened, and three years later the Wilhelmina Gasthuis closed down.

What happened then seems to be a kind of ritual in Amsterdam. The city authorities want to close something down. The local residents, energetically supported by artists, protest, and in the end agreement is reached on a compromise solution. In this case that meant cautious renovation and repurposing of the old hospital site for residential use, for offices and for leisure facilities. Of which the most surprising is Ski-Inn, the only artificial ski slope in Amsterdam. It has to be admitted that you would not seriously recommend anyone to make a trip to Amsterdam to go skiing, of all things, but if you are there, it is worth taking a look at the place. The artificial slope consists of conveyor belts large enough for four skiers. The speed of the belts can be changed, thus simulating different levels of difficulty.

To be fair it has to be said that even an outstandingly talented skier will only make modest progress here. When it comes down to it, the whole thing is little more than a deluxe version of a beginners' slope. Those who construct such a facility and those who venture to ski on it must love the sport very, very much.

Address Wg-Plein 281, NL-1054 SE Amsterdam (West) | Getting there Tram 3, 12 to Overtoom | Hours Mon–Sat 10am–11pm, Sun 10am–6pm, for further information see www.ski-inn.nl | Tip Closer to the hearts of Dutch sports fans is the Jaap Eden ice-skating rink at Radioweg 64. The season usually lasts from October to March.

106__ The Windmill in Amstelpark

Don Quixote's best friend

Windmills are believed to have existed in Holland since at least 1180. Of the classic Dutch windmills that look like towers and have been reproduced on billions of postcards and in travel brochures, not many remain. Some maintain that there are only four such mills. And one of the last survivors can be admired in Amstelpark.

It was the discovery of steam power at the start of the Industrial Revolution that finished off the windmills, but until the days of their decline they were ingenious miracles of technology (according to the state of the art in those days), whose operation was continually being refined. The design of the sails was improved to catch more wind, and then someone hit on the idea of placing a mill on a rotating axis, so that the whole structure could be swivelled to align with the direction from which the wind was blowing. And if there was nothing better to do, you could get on a horse and charge at the mill carrying a lance, as Don Quixote once did, and see what happened.

Usually nothing happened. Of course all kinds of things could be processed by a mill, but in the Netherlands they were so common because they performed a further task that was almost as important as providing bread. The mills powered pumps that drained the land so that it could be farmed. In the area around Zaan (a little town to the north of Amsterdam on the narrow strip of land that goes up to the Friesian Islands) windmills were once thick on the ground. There seems to have been no kind of work for which they were not suited. They sawed wood that had been imported from Scandinavia for shipbuilding. Mills ground up rags for the paper industry and crushed linseed to produce the oil that was used by dyers. Mills drained the water to create polders, and of course they also did the job for which they are best known: they ground cereals to make flour.

Address Europaboulevard, NL-1083 Amsterdam (Zuid/Buienveldert) | Getting there
Bus 62 to Weerdestein | Hours Viewable from the outside only | Tip In Amstelpark there
is a miniature railway for children and a crazy-golf course (for kids or adults).

107 __ The Woonbootmuseum

A home on the water

Even a short trip along the canals demonstrates beyond doubt that houseboats are part and parcel of everyday life in Amsterdam. Many of them are more than just a weekend home or accommodation for the summer season. Some residents of Amsterdam have spent their whole lives on a houseboat. This has lots of charm, but also a downside. The space is limited on a boat, however generously it was planned – and most were not conceived as spacious homes. And in a boat made of wood, even when it is moored by the quayside, you are exposed to the elements much more directly than in a brick-built house.

On the other hand, this closeness to nature is also the great advantage of a houseboat. Several people who grew up on boats have told me with a broad smile how, when they were children, they could climb straight out of the cabin window and step onto the icy surface of the canal to go skating if the winter was cold enough for a thick layer of ice to freeze. Perhaps those who grew up on a houseboat experience the gentle rocking and rolling that can never be avoided completely on the water as a state of affairs that is not somehow unsettling, but as conveying a sense of security and well-being. The world and the home are then a big cradle that rocks you to sleep gently every evening.

All of this is true even without considering that the residents of houseboats will be among the beneficiaries of climate change, if the polar ice-caps really do melt one day.

In the Woonbootmuseum (Houseboat Museum) you can get a close-up look at this unusual world. The Hendrika Maria was built in 1914 and served for 50 years as a freighter carrying bulk materials. In those years, the captain's family spent most of their lives on board. After the ship was taken out of service, she was a proper houseboat for a further 20 years, until in 1997 she was converted into a museum.

Address Prinsengracht 296K, NL-1016 HW Amsterdam (Centrum/Jordaan) | **Getting there** Tram 10 or 17 to Elandsgracht | **Hours** Daily 10am–5pm | **Tip** Maroxidien (Prins Hendrikkade 534) is a houseboat that has been converted into a hotel, the right address for anyone who would like unconventional accommodation.

108__The Women's House
No Man's Land

The building on Nieuwe Herengracht (New Men's Canal) had been empty for quite some time when a group of people occupied it in 1973. Subsequently the address was renamed Nieuwe Vrouwengracht (New Women's Canal), and the building became the first house for women in the Netherlands. The second wave of feminism was approaching its climax, and women wanted to have a place where they could be themselves.

A wide variety of activities arose in the house. There were discussion groups, and women taught each other to dance tango. DIY courses were held. At the bar you could order herbal teas that helped with menstruation pains. Again and again there were heated debates about diverse topics. For example, 'all women are subjugated, even by their own husbands'. Campaign months were announced, including a sex strike called Purple September with the motto 'Don't go to bed with the oppressor'. At night, teams went out to put up posters, protests were held against beauty contests, and witches' nights were organised against sexual violence. There was a feminist film production, and the women's publisher De Bonte Was is still based at this address.

Ultimately it could be said that all of this was about respect, even if the never-ending debates were not always characterised by mutual respect and admiration. This was definitely not the case. In the women's house, observers were unwelcome, and only women were admitted to the premises. This fact is not without irony, as the building had once been home to a school for technical apprentices – who were all male. Some of them later wanted to take a look inside their old place of training, but they were not allowed through the door. And some of them may then have recalled that while they did their apprenticeships there, the only females who were permitted in the sacred halls were the daughters of the caretaker.

Address Nieuwe Herengracht 95, NL-1011 RX Amsterdam (Centrum) | Getting there
Tram 7, 9 or 14 to Meester Visserplein | Hours Viewable from the outside only | Tip
Find out more about the spirit of these years in the Electric Ladyland museum, Tweede
Leliedwarsstraat 5.

109__ The Wood Sawyer

Don't saw the branch you're sitting on

It may already be history, but Koninginnedag was not really the birthday of Queen Beatrix, just as in Britain the Queen's official birthday is not the date she was born. The Dutch monarch simply adopted the date of her predecessor's anniversary, because it seemed sensible: the weather is better for a celebration, and apart from that you can sleep off the after-effects on 1 May, a public holiday. In fact Queen Beatrix was born on 31 January, and on the evening of that day in 1989 an unknown artist placed a work in a tree in the Leidsebosje wood. It represents a man sawing a branch.

As this image, at a cursory glance, seems to be realistic (the artist was clearly not only a man with a mission but also a skilled craftsman), some time passed before it was regarded as a work of art. In Amsterdam they have, after all, seen more remarkable things than a man who stands in a tree in broad daylight and starts to saw. To this day no one knows what the artist is called, and so the name of the work is also unknown. Over the years, the name 'houtzagertje' or 'boomzagertje' (i.e. wood or tree sawyer) has gained acceptance.

The resonance in the media was huge, and in the course of time new works by unknown creators appeared in the city. But what is the artist saying in this work? Is he (or she?) telling us that humanity should take care and not saw off the branch that it is sitting on? Or that people who always want to find a meaning in everything should be cut down? Was it a coded message to the queen, telling her not to snore? Or saying it would have been better if Rembrandt had been a lumberjack? No matter – you can find serious arguments for any interpretation. And perhaps the artist only wanted to make us talk about art again and to get people to take a closer look at their surroundings. If so, he or she more than achieved this aim.

Address Leidsebosje, NL-1054 Amsterdam (West) | Getting there Tram 1 to Eerste Constanijn Huygensstraat | Tip A further anonymous work on Waterlooplein depicts a violinist, half sunk into the ground.

110___Xaviera's Happy House B&B

Sleep in the bed of a sex goddess

The beginning, at least, of the biography of Vera de Vries reads like the description of a role from a play by Bertolt Brecht. She was born in Surabaya (Indonesia), where her father was in charge of the local hospital. Her mother was a model with French ancestry.

Vera went to South Africa, and later ended up in New York, having fallen in love. When the relationship ended, she started a career as a call girl in the 1970s. She wrote of her experiences in a book called *The Happy Hooker*, which was a media sensation and made her world-famous under her pen name Xaviera Hollander. Several films were made about her, and there was even a musical (though it has to be said that this is not so extraordinary, as there is hardly a story that the Dutch will not make into a musical). On top of that, for many years she provided tips about sex for a men's magazine. Xaviera Hollander thus defined an image of her profession that is represented in her home country today by women such as Kim Holland and Bobbi Eden – doubtless with a similarly professional attitude, but without the cosmopolitan glamour that surrounded their predecessor in the late 20th century.

Today, Xaviera runs a small guesthouse in the south of Amsterdam. It is characterised by a friendly atmosphere and tolerance. Everybody is welcome here, regardless of their sexual preferences, and regardless of whether they arrive on a motorbike or in a wheelchair. Of course, pets are allowed, and – something that amounts to a sensation nowadays – in some of the rooms you can even smoke. Her husband is a great chef, and will happily cook you a delicious meal.

Those who are interested can approach the lady of the house: she organises seminars and tells the participants stories that draw on her extensive past experiences. But you can also come here just to get a bed for the night.

Address Stadionweg 17, NL-1077 RV Amsterdam (Zuid) | **Getting there** Tram 5 or 24 to Apollolaan/Stadionweg | **Hours** Reservations: +31 (20)6733934, information at www.xavierahollander.com | **Tip** Once a place to stay where no one would willingly spend the night, now an art gallery: the former nuclear bunker at Vondelpark 8a.

111_ The Zevenlandenhuizen

The European Union, in miniature

In 1894, a world exhibition was held in Antwerp. For the occasion, the architect Tjeerd Kuipers built a street with seven houses in Amsterdam to a commission from Samuel van Eeghen, a wealthy banker and politician.

Each of the seven was to represent a different European style. Kuipers was born in the mid-19th century and lived for almost 100 years, until the mid-20th. This means that he repeatedly witnessed how the great idea of a peaceful and harmonious Europe came to nothing.

But in the 1890s there was still hope that tensions and conflicts between the European powers could be solved by peaceful means. These expectations were not met in their entirety, to put it mildly, but that should not stop us from taking a closer look at his buildings.

The house at number 20 represents the German Romanesque style. Number 22 is meant to be reminiscent of a French château on the Loire, number 24 of the Moorish architecture that was widespread in Spain. Number 26 was inspired by an Italian palazzo, number 28 by Russian cathedrals with their onion domes. Number 30 was built in the domestic Dutch manner, in the style popular there during the Renaissance. Last but not least, number 30A looks like an English cottage.

It is not known how Kuipers' idea was received. Today this little street makes a cute impression. It has a touch of Disneyland or a theme park. And then you could question whether these replicas are accurate down to the last detail … but we'll leave that judgement to the experts. For visitors to the city, this architectural row certainly makes a change and provides a surprise. But the architect's idea was not imitated. Kuipers was mainly employed as a church architect. In the course of his career he designed and built more than 50 places of worship, most of which no longer exist. But with these houses, a street showing a miniature version of Europe, the architect gained immortality.

Address Roemer Visscherstraat, NL-1054 Amsterdam (West) | Getting there Tram 1 to Stadhouderskade | Hours Viewable from the outside only | Tip The fast Thalys train takes only two hours to Brussels, where you can see the heart of the real European Union in action. If you want.

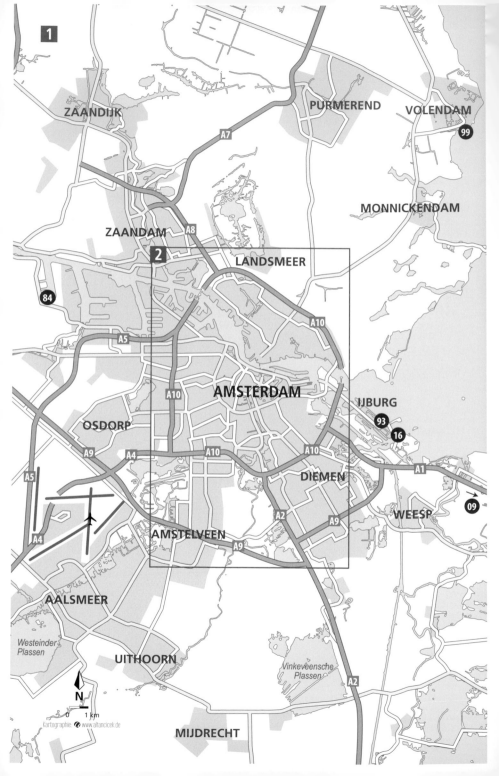

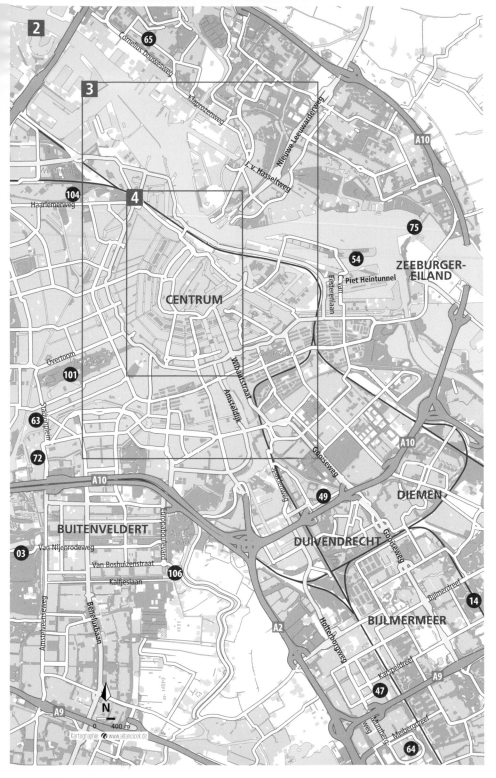

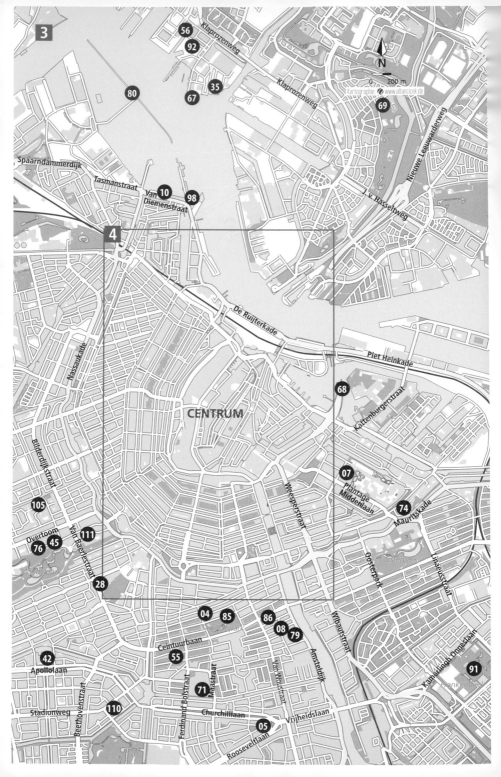

Lucia Jay von Seldeneck,
Carolin Huder, Verena Eidel
**111 PLACES IN BERLIN
THAT YOU SHOULDN'T MISS**
ISBN 978-3-95451-208-9

Rüdiger Liedtke
**111 PLACES IN MUNICH
THAT YOU SHOULDN'T MISS**
ISBN 978-3-95451-222-5

Frank McNally
**111 PLACES IN DUBLIN
THAT YOU SHOULDN'T MISS**
ISBN 978-3-95451-649-0

Rike Wolf
**111 PLACES IN HAMBURG
THAT YOU SHOULDN'T MISS**
ISBN 978-3-95451-234-8

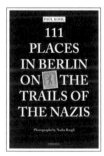

Paul Kohl
**111 PLACES IN BERLIN
ON THE TRAIL OF THE NAZIS**
ISBN 978-3-95451-323-9

Peter Eickhoff
**111 PLACES IN VIENNA
THAT YOU SHOULDN'T MISS**
ISBN 978-3-95451-206-5

Sharon Fernandes
**111 PLACES IN NEW DELHI
THAT YOU MUST NOT MISS**
ISBN 978-3-95451-648-3

Sally Asher, Michael Murphy
**111 PLACES IN NEW ORLEANS
THAT YOU MUST NOT MISS**
ISBN 978-3-95451-645-2

Gordon Streisand
**111 PLACES IN MIAMI
AND THE KEYS
THAT YOU MUST NOT MISS**
ISBN 978-3-95451-644-5

Dirk Engelhardt
**111 PLACES IN BARCELONA
THAT YOU MUST NOT MISS**
ISBN 978-3-95451-353-6

Rüdiger Liedtke
**111 PLACES ON MALLORCA
THAT YOU SHOULDN'T MISS**
ISBN 978-3-95451-281-2

Marcus X. Schmid
**111 PLACES IN ISTANBUL
THAT YOU MUST NOT MISS**
ISBN 978-3-95451-423-6

Stefan Spath
**111 PLACES IN SALZBURG
THAT YOU SHOULDN'T MISS**
ISBN 978-3-95451-230-0

Ralf Nestmeyer
**111 PLACES IN PROVENCE
THAT YOU MUST NOT MISS**
ISBN 978-3-95451-422-9

Christiane Bröcker,
Babette Schröder
**111 PLACES IN STOCKHOLM
THAT YOU MUST NOT MISS**
ISBN 978-3-95451-459-5

Beate C. Kirchner
**111 PLACES IN FLORENCE
AND NORTHERN TUSCANY
THAT YOU MUST NOT MISS**
ISBN 978-3-95451-613-1

Floriana Petersen, Steve Werney
**111 PLACES IN SAN FRANCISCO
THAT YOU MUST NOT MISS**
ISBN 978-3-95451-609-4

Ralf Nestmeyer
**111 PLACES ON THE
FRENCH RIVIERA
THAT YOU MUST NOT MISS**
ISBN 978-3-95451-612-4

Gerd Wolfgang Sievers
**111 PLACES IN VENICE
THAT YOU MUST NOT MISS**
ISBN 978-3-95451-460-1

Petra Sophia Zimmermann
**111 PLACES IN VERONA
AND LAKE GARDA THAT
YOU MUST NOT MISS**
ISBN 978-3-95451-611-7

Rüdiger Liedtke,
Laszlo Trankovits
**111 PLACES IN CAPE TOWN
THAT YOU MUST NOT MISS**
ISBN 978-3-95451-610-0

Gillian Tait
**111 PLACES IN EDINBURGH
THAT YOU SHOULDN'T MISS**
ISBN 978-3-95451-883-8

Laurel Moglen, Julia Posey
**111 PLACES IN LOS ANGELES
THAT YOU SHOULDN'T MISS**
ISBN 978-3-95451-884-5

Giulia Castelli Gattinara,
Mario Verin
**111 PLACES IN MILAN
THAT YOU MUST NOT MISS**
ISBN 978-3-95451-331-4

John Sykes
**111 PLACES IN LONDON
THAT YOU SHOULDN'T MISS**
ISBN 978-3-95451-346-8

Julian Treuherz,
Peter de Figueiredo
**111 PLACES IN LIVERPOOL
THAT YOU SHOULDN'T MISS**
ISBN 978-3-95451-769-5

Jo-Anne Elikann
**111 PLACES IN NEW YORK
THAT YOU MUST NOT MISS**
ISBN 978-3-95451-052-8

Matěj Černý, Marie Peřinová
111 PLACES IN PRAGUE
THAT YOU SHOULDN'T MISS
ISBN 978-3-7408-0144-1

Sybil Canac, Renée Grimaud,
Katia Thomas
111 PLACES IN PARIS THAT
YOU SHOULDN'T MISS
ISBN 978-3-7408-0159-5

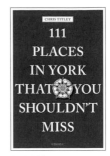

Chris Titley
111 PLACES IN YORK THAT
YOU SHOULDN'T MISS
ISBN 978-3-95451-768-8

Kathrin Bielfeldt,
Raymond Wong, Jürgen Bürger
111 PLACES IN HONG KONG
THAT YOU SHOULDN'T MISS
ISBN 978-3-95451-936-1

Justin Postlethwaite
111 PLACES IN BATH THAT
YOU SHOULDN'T MISS
ISBN 978-3-7408-0146-5

Rosalind Horton,
Sally Simmons, Guy Snape
111 PLACES IN CAMBRIDGE
THAT YOU SHOULDN'T MISS
ISBN 978-3-7408-0147-2

Joe DiStefano, Clay Williams
111 PLACES IN QUEENS
THAT YOU MUST NOT MISS
ISBN 978-3-7408-0020-8

Allison Robicelli, John Dean
111 PLACES IN BALTIMORE
THAT YOU MUST NOT MISS
ISBN 978-3-7408-0158-8

Elisabeth Larsen
111 PLACES IN THE
TWIN CITIES THAT
YOU MUST NOT MISS
ISBN 978-3-7408-0029-1

The author

Thomas Fuchs is a writer. Amsterdam played a leading part in his first novel, *Grenzverkehr* (*Border Traffic*; 2009), but that was not his only point of contact with the Netherlands. He previously worked as a joke writer for the Dutch comedian Rudi Carrell and was the correspondent in Germany of the unfortunately short-lived Dutch satirical magazine *PIM* (*Politiek Incorrect Magazine*). In 2012, his biography of Mark Twain, *Ein Mann von Welt* (*A Man of the World*), was published, and in 2013 his first historical novel, *Arminius – Kampf gegen Rom* (*Arminius – The Battle Against Rome*).

General Transportation Notice

In 2018, the North-South Line of the Amsterdam metro will finally open after a long period of construction. The city administration wants as many Amsterdamers as possible to ride the subway and therefore plans to discontinue tram lines or provide new routes. Many Amsterdamers are very attached to their trams and will most likely push to retain these lines. The outcome is not yet clear, so make sure to check en.gvb.nl for the latest updates and directions.